> # the Morality MAZE

Two things fill the mind with
ever new and increasing
admiration and awe—
the starry heavens above
and the moral law within.

Immanuel Kant
(1724–1804)

the Morality MAZE

AN INTRODUCTION TO MORAL ECOLOGY

Neil M. Daniels

Prometheus Books
Buffalo, New York

Published 1991 by Prometheus Books

The Morality Maze: An Introduction to Moral Ecology. Copyright © 1991 by Neil M. Daniels. All rights reserved. No part of this publication may be reproduced, stored in a retrieval system, transmitted in any form or by any means, electronic, mechanical, photocopying, recording, or otherwise, without prior written permission of the publisher, except in the case of brief quotations embodied in critical articles and reviews. Inquiries should be addressed to Prometheus Books, 700 East Amherst Street, Buffalo, New York 14215, 716-837-2475/FAX 716-835-6901.

95 94 93 92 91   5 4 3 2 1

Library of Congress Cataloging-in-Publication Data

Daniels, Neil M.
    The morality maze : an introduction to moral ecology / Neil M. Daniels.
       p.   cm.
    Includes bibliographical references.
    ISBN 0-87975-697-7
    1. Ethics. 2. Human ecology—Moral and ethical aspects. I. Title.
BJ1012.D28.   1992
171'.7—dc20   91-18489
                                                                                           CIP

Printed in the United States of America on acid-free paper.

Acknowledgments

My references to and accreditation of all individuals mentioned here and in the general text of the book are not meant to imply that they endorse any of my ideas, my interpretations of their writings, or any of my concepts or opinions. I am solely responsible for the subject matter and viewpoints expressed.

Those who bring together the ideas of others to produce still other ideas accumulate both indebtedness and gratitude. When that happens, as it does to some degree with all writers, it is appropriate to give credit and thanks to all who have supplied materials, help, influence, and encouragement. I want to first recognize several authors whose ideas undergird my moral theorizing, and I want to thank those who personally assisted and supported me.

The eminent psychologist Erich Fromm published *Man For Himself,* his comprehensive humanistic theory of morality, in 1947. This fascinating work provided me with many alternative ways of understanding and evaluating moral behavior. In my chapter 21, "On Being Your Own Moral Expert," I use Fromm's theory of productive love in illustrating applications of moral ecology principles.

The importance of the facts of biological necessity in moral thought was brought home to me by biologist Paul R. Ehrlich in his 1968 work *The Population Bomb.* My interest in a biological basis for a theory of morality was stimulated by Ehrlich's arresting presentation of the ecological threat of overpopulation.

It should be generally recognized today that the moral analysis of an act must thoroughly consider the state of the human ecosystem (i.e., the state of the actor's situation) at the time the act was committed. This principle was thoroughly described and illustrated by Joseph Fletcher, a theologian and moral philosopher, in his book *Situation Ethics,* published in 1966. The principle was also given impetus by the biologist Garrett Hardin in his article titled "The Tragedy of the Commons" (*Science,* 13 December 1968), and his book titled *Exploring New Ethics For Survival,* published in 1968. The ideas of these writers were never far from my mind while I was working on this book.

The Morality Maze advances a new way of examining and analyzing the nature of morality. The new way demands that we rework our perception of property; that we expand its ordinary language definition to include our lives, our derivative thoughts and ideas, and all else that we create and accumulate in the course of acquiring the requisites of life and its fulfillment. The new way also demands that we reject the untoward view that property is more likely to be a source of evil than a fount of morality. Actually, there is no other reason than the very existence of property that we cherish morality.

I am indebted to Andrew J. Galambos,* a Southern California astrophysicist and scientific thinker who, so far as I can determine, originated what I call the theory of the contiguity of property, upon which I frequently rely in constructing the theory of moral ecology set forth herein. When I first heard Galambos state his theory of property at a seminar in 1972, I realized that I now had the scientific base for understanding the moral dynamics of a human ecological system. Galambos's radical concept of property leads to a similarly innovative definition of freedom.

I have elaborated on Galambos's concepts of property and freedom in chapter 19 on "Property, Profit, and Morals" and in chapter 23 on "Freedom." My encounter with Galambos in 1972, when I was on the verge of retiring, gave me a welcome intellectual jolt. This, and later encounters, added to and shifted around the furnishings of my mind. I recall these experiences with pleasure and gratitude. The Galambos concepts mentioned above are but two of dozens to be found in his work that systematically diagnose and prescribe for the precarious predicament of modern humankind.

My son, David N. Daniels, M.D., Professor of Clinical Psychiatry at Stanford University, gave me the sort of close support a writer needs:

---

*Andrew J. Galambos is the founder and director of the Liberal Institute of Natural Science and Technology.

kind and positive criticism, helpful suggestions, sincere encouragement and, as a bonus, careful first-draft editing of the entire manuscript. I deeply appreciate all the time he so generously donated over the four-year course of the writing process. The reader must be made aware that we do not concur in all of my ideas, theories, and opinions. This book is not a joint work. I alone am responsible for its final form and content.

My daughter-in-law, Judy Daniels, will always have my deepest gratitude, not only for typing the entire manuscript through several revisions, but for maintaining a cheerful and upbeat attitude toward me throughout the whole ordeal.

For putting up with my unkempt workroom for the duration of the writing, all the while making me feel welcome in my own home, my wife, Billie, deserves all the love and appreciation I can give.

A few other people gave me help along the way. I owe praise and thanks to Keith Tremelling and John Minick for editorial work, and to Denise Daniels and W. B. Hubbell for special contributions to the project.

For his fine tuning of the manuscript, I am deeply indebted to my editor, Steven L. Mitchell, of Prometheus Books. His painstaking attention to details and his wise counsel have enhanced the form and content of the book.

Contents

Acknowledgments   5

PART ONE: THE MORALITY MAZE

    1. The Purpose of this Book: What It Is All About   13
    2. Defining Morals, Ethics, and Related Terms   15
    3. Swaying Moral Opinion   21
    4. Developing Moral Knowledge   25
    5. The Morality Maze   31
    6. Roadblocks to Moral Understanding   35

PART TWO: MORALITY: ITS ORIGIN AND DEVELOPMENT

    7. In the Beginning   41
    8. Moral Development among Primitives   45
    9. The Role of Religion and Government in the History of Morals   49
    10. Human Nature as a Shaper of Morals   57
    11. Genetic Factors in the Roots of Morality   61

10   The Morality Maze

    12. Intellect Versus Emotion, Belief, and Habit
        in Human Nature   67

PART THREE: MORAL PRINCIPLES AND MODELS
                  FOR OUR TIMES

    13. Is a Simple, Comprehensive System of Morals Possible?   75
    14. The Human Environment   79
    15. The Moral Lessons of Catastrophes   89
    16. Extending Our Environmental Reach   97
    17. Life Flow and Life Cycles   105
    18. Matters of Life and Death   131
    19. Property, Profit, and Morals   141
    20. The Ecology of Morals   153

PART FOUR: CONQUERING MORAL PROBLEMS

    21. On Being Our Own Moral Expert   163
    22. Rights   189
    23. Freedom   207

Index   225

Part One
The Morality Maze

1

The Purpose of this Book: What It Is All About

This is a book about morals: what they are, how they came to be, the purposes they serve, how we can use them to improve the quality of our own lives and that of others, how morals have been passed from one generation to another, how they have failed and succeeded, and how they can be used effectively in the improvement of society.

I planned this book as a guide to new moral concepts for our times, a book that will give everyday men and women a practical working knowledge of moral principles of sufficient substance to make it possible for them to analyze for themselves the moral problems of today. I have striven to identify and separate verifiable moral principles from the hodgepodge of beliefs, customs, conventions, taboos, sins, political opinions, and pompous reports of public policy makers, all of which frequently pass for morality in the media. Further, throughout this book I shall call attention to how we can protect ourselves from being manipulated by moralistic propaganda. Also, what we learn will enable us to hold our own in discussions of moral issues.

Scholars in history, moral philosophy, religion, and law will realize that a full recognition of the contributions of their special fields to moral knowledge is beyond the scope of this book. In the last six thousand years, an enormous literature on morals has accumulated. I have dealt lightly with moral history and its literary landmarks, most of which have little bearing on my approach to moral thought.

Specializing in moral phenomena, as I am doing herein, courts the danger of playing down the significance of all else that results from and leads to human behavior. Without the discovery of moral principles, we would not be here. Morals are important; however, we do not live *for* them but *because of* them. Fortunately, life offers much more, but probably nothing more important to our well-being.

The basic theme of this book is an ecological theory of morals based on the biological facts of our existence, our perpetual needs, our dependence on our inner environment of self and our outer environment of others, and the natural world. Morality arises in the interactions of human beings within the human ecological system. Moral behavior is the way humans function together to make and use an ecosystem to fulfill their biological requisites. I shall gradually reveal the science of human ecology through a comprehensive series of practical illustrations drawn from contemporary life. I shall then explain the rather specialized knowledge needed as we proceed together.

After a few introductory paragraphs, Part One takes up the definitions of moral terminology as they will be used in this book, and I make important changes in the vocabulary of traditional moral writing. The several chapters that follow cover an assortment of tricks designed to sway moral opinion; expressions that are palmed off as moral principles; the morality maze, mainly constructed by government, politics, law, and religion; and cultural obstacles that block moral understanding.

Part Two, entitled "The Origins and Shaping of Morality," sketches the origins of moral behavior and traces its history, highlighting the major factors that shaped moral evolution: for example, human nature, genetics, the interplay of human intellect and emotions, and belief and habit.

Part Three, "Moral Principles and Models for Our Times," deals with the difficulties of creating a science of moral ecology; it consists of eight chapters, each one of which explores a major domain of human ecology and moral behavior. I consider this part of the work to be its centerpiece. The whole of what I have to say about the ecology of morals is contained there.

Part Four, "Conquering Moral Problems," is a practical demonstration of the application of moral ecology principles to the solution of a number of tough moral problems and dilemmas.

2

Defining Morals, Ethics, and Related Terms

Over the course of history, writers on morals and ethics have developed a specialized terminology. It has become one of the most troublesome tangles in the morality maze. I am going to handle this tangle by skirting around it. Fortunately, my approach to morals and ethics makes it feasible to banish many common terms used in moral philosophy and in everyday conversation. In this way we can avoid many tiresome definitions of shopworn terms by simply ignoring them. For example, I shall make no references to these outmoded terms: *virtue* and *vice, good* and *evil,* and *right* and *wrong*.

Other common terms used in moral discourse can be downgraded in importance or eliminated. We shall closely examine the terms *fairness* and *unfairness, justice* and *injustice,* and the tricky words *values* and *equality*. The restricted use of habitual moral terminology will sharpen rather than blur moral thought. The frequently misused and misunderstood terms *rights* and *freedom* are major topics. I briefly introduce them in this chapter, reserving their detailed analysis for later.

I see no point in starting out with a dictionary-like definition of morals. We have our own personal ideas concerning the meaning of the concept, and I want readers to feel comfortable about theirs. This book in its entirety is concerned with expanding our conception and understanding of morals, so with no great difficulty we will find ourselves continually redefining the subject matter of morals as we move along.

We shall be constantly on the lookout for common misconceptions about morality in both its history and its substance. Occasionally I may say something that is at odds with what others have learned long ago. It would be natural for this to disturb some readers. While my aim is to present only verifiable facts, I lay no claim to being infallible. I therefore encourage all who read this book to be skeptical concerning my remarks. It is hard for people to change long-standing beliefs and it is not unwise to question. It is vitally important to have an open and receptive mind. If readers come to my discussion with this attitude of free and open inquiry, then I will be satisfied of receiving a fair hearing.

A common misconception is that morals have something to do with forbidden forms of sexual activity. This interpretation parallels the Judeo-Christian doctrine that all sexual expression practiced outside marriage is sinful or immoral. Many cultures do not view sex, which is a biological phenomenon, as intrinsically immoral whether inside or outside of marriage. Nevertheless, the word *moral(s)* has long been confused with and contaminated by social and religious prejudice, political opinion, conventional rules of conduct, statutory laws and emotional motivations, that to a great extent constitute what I call the morality maze. Some of the most brilliant people have been trapped in it. A famous twentieth-century psychologist stated that moralists are probably sick personalities who preach morals to absolve their own immorality. Of course, what the psychologist was really talking about was the dubious sexual and family-life prohibitions that should have been laid at the doorstep of convention, religion, and law rather than at the doorstep of morality.

I shall now turn briefly to the variants of the root terms *moral* and *ethic,* which are regarded as synonyms. The following sentence will serve as a starting point for highlighting linguistic difficulties: "A moral or ethical act promotes human well-being." Note that *ethical* replaces *ethic,* the synonym of *moral.* In this illustration, *moral* and *ethical* are both used as adjectives modifying *act. Moral* functions as a singular noun or as an adjective. The term *ethics* is also construed as a noun as in the study of moral philosophy. It would be correct to say "a new *ethic* or a new *moral* for our times," thus using the singular form of each noun. *Morals* or *ethics* in everyday usage appear to be interchangeable terms. Here is a list of interchangeable terms based on the twins morals-ethics: *moralist-ethicist, morality-ethicality, moralistic-ethicalistic.*

Several prefixes are commonly joined to *moral* as in *amoral,* meaning not possessing any knowledge of morals, neither moral nor immoral; *im-*

moral, the opposite of moral; *unmoral,* similar to amoral plus ignorance of morality; and *nonmoral,* similar to amoral, also a subject that is unrelated to moral or ethical concepts.

Ethics is usually defined as a code or the standards of conduct. Individual items of such a code may or may not be moral, as is the case with laws, many of which are actually immoral. In modern usage, ethics and morals may still be *regarded* as synonymous, but they don't have exactly the same meanings. In the late nineteenth and early twentieth centuries, ethics was thought of as the science of morals. I cannot find evidence that ethics has attained the posture of a science, much less becoming a science of morals.

The word *ethics* has won a secure place as a label for the rules and regulations of various types of organizations, such as fraternal, business, educational, governmental, religious, and professional groups, each of which may have a code of ethics to which members are bound. The penalty for disobeying the code can be quite severe; e.g., expulsion from the organization. Such codes range over matters of internal relations of members to external relations to clients, patients, patrons, customers, and the like. Individual ethical rules may deal with serious problems of a moral nature, such as harming patients, swindling clients, phony guarantees, grand theft, sexual harassment, and so on. Also, instructions may be laid down for mannerly conduct, explaining interest charges, warning clients of company policy changes, and innumerable others.

Under the labels *morals* and *ethics* we have two separate but operationally related categories of subject matter, each with separate vocabularies. The indiscriminate intermixing of terms from these two subjects undermines clarity and enhances confusion, or so it seems to me. I also believe that the boundaries of moral thought are more easily defined than those of ethics. Therefore, in the interest of simplicity and clarity, I shall strictly limit my use of ethics and related terms in the balance of this book.

The words *fair* and *unfair, fairness* and *unfairness* are used most frequently in connection with games and contests of all kinds. In sports and other types of recreation, it is important to abide by cut and dried rules. To do otherwise would spoil the pleasure of other players. Participants may be asked to leave the game or they may be required to suffer a penalty, all of which may be stipulated in the rules. Cheaters will be accused of unfairness, or assailed with some form of punitive aggression. Games are a kind of microcosm of life itself: business is often viewed and played as a game, as is marriage to some extent. If the players break the rules too often—if they cheat and treat each other unfairly—a player may bow out of the game via divorce or by handing in a resignation.

In the 1984 United States presidential campaign, the Democrats unwisely chose to push a fairness-unfairness issue, accusing the Republicans of unfair treatment of the "disadvantaged." Fingers could be pointed with impunity because no specified rules of fairness and unfairness exist for the game of politics. When the Democratic vice-presidential candidate went a step beyond unfairness and accused President Reagan of being both immoral and un-Christian, she found herself in trouble with her own political party. The shift from using a weak word like *unfair* to a strong word like *immoral* manifests a real difference. It is like the difference between a slap on the wrist and a sock on the jaw.

We cannot fool around with the word *morals*. Moral elements are not matters of opinion, individual taste, and prejudice. They are concrete and stable and have definite meanings. If we accuse a person of immorality, we had better be able to prove it because we may well wind up in court for libel. Such is not the case with *fairness*. It has so many meanings: fairhaired, a fair defeat, fair weather, fair and square, and dozens more. *Unjust* is like *immoral,* and *justice* like *fair,* in common parlance.

Injustice is easier to define and to illustrate than *justice*. To sustain an irreparable loss without restitution is a characteristic of all injustice. Being blinded, raped, robbed, taken hostage, defrauded and the like, all without recourse or restitution of any kind are injustices. Even if the culprit who committed the crime is caught, tried, and punished, the victim suffers injustice. The victim's loss cannot be fully restored. Justice, the opposite of injustice, cannot be fully obtained, even though the criminal is said to have been "brought to justice." The word *justice,* like *fairness,* has many meanings.

A definition of a *right* or *rights* must consider the fact that we have no natural or God-given rights. It is one thing for evangelicals to proclaim the "rights of the unborn," but quite another matter to obtain a constitutional amendment conferring such rights on the unborn. A right does not come into existence in a democracy by mere proclamation. A legal right is created by the legislative process of government. It is conferred, we might say, by government upon its citizens and backed by all legal forces at the disposal of the political regime. Rights are more fully discussed in later chapters.

Since the writing of the Declaration of Independence, the word *equal* has been a part of American political speech. In science and mathematics, it has a precise theoretical function; in politics, law, and society it has little use except to obscure issues. No two people are equal, nor do they have equal opportunity in regard to anything. Too many organismic and situational variables exist. It would improve political and moral thinking if the words *equal* and *unequal* were abandoned. After all, in politics and social life they do not mean any more or less than *fair* or *unfair* and could be regarded as synonymous with the latter.

Another tricky word is *value*. When we say the value of a dollar changes, we mean that the kinds or types of things we can purchase with it have changed. The value of a baby's portrait is in the great emotional significance it holds for the parents, but such a painting would have no commercial value as a picture offered for sale. The cost of a building may go up in price with inflation but its functional value may not change at all. I contend that it is questionable to speak of moral or ethical values. Who made the valuation? For what purpose? Value is a measure, but what is the unit of measurement? Obviously, value is a vague term. It is ideally suited to political maneuvering, where I for one do not wish to be identified with a precisely stated political or moral position. I shall therefore avoid using moral value because it suggests that morals are subjective and relative, as people who have not read Part Three frequently believe. *Value* in moral discourse is what someone says it is and no more useful than the word *opinion*.

Freedom is not an easy word to define yet it is used frequently by Americans, especially journalists and politicians. In 1972, I began asking people to define freedom, and I have yet to hear any straight answers to the question. Ask friends and acquaintances and the answers come slowly and hesitantly. Some people refer to the freedoms mentioned in the First Amendment to the U.S. Constitution. Others mention freedom to choose, to travel, to divorce, to change occupations, and then run out of things to say. Actually, all of these examples employ the word *freedom* so they are not really definitions. Attempt to define freedom without using the word itself, or wait and read the definition in Part Four. A warning to those who are tempted to fudge their definition: liberty is a synonym for freedom.

I shall briefly comment on some other terms that can be confusing in the discussion of morality. They are *harm, hurt, injure, coerce,* and *use of force*. All are used in describing both moral and immoral acts. *Harm,* in a social sense, is not necessarily immoral. To harm, injure, or hurt another person physically or emotionally is regarded as immoral, but we might do these same things in capturing or restraining those who break the law. It is obvious, then, that the term *harm* is neither moral nor immoral. In interpreting its moral status, we must consider the total field of the human interactions of which harm is a factor. This principle applies to the terms *hurt, injure,* and *use of force*. It is a mistake to think of these terms as always associated with immorality.

3

Swaying Moral Opinion

The morality maze is a dangerous place and we are familiar with its dangers, such as terrorism, hijacking, hostage taking, street crime, assassination, and child abuse, to mention just a few. We understand these dangers, but we can only partially control them. More hidden but every bit as treacherous is the use of language as a means of social and political control. Lies and misinformation are common enough but not difficult to detect and countermand. Propaganda, the education of "the other side," is effective especially if repeated frequently by an agent we trust. It can complicate the moral decision-making process. However, more concealed and insidious is *word magic*—the use of a word or phrase by people in public life to cast doubt on the character and thoughts of opponents or competitors without offering substantial proof.

A few examples of word magic will help us spot it in the media. The word *insensitive* is thrown like a hand grenade at political adversaries, indicating that the person or group so called is callous, heartless, stingy, and the like. Meg Greenfield, columnist for *Newsweek,* points out that writers and political speakers shy away from using the word *wrong.*[*] A candidate, for example, may be stupid but not wrong. "Bad" is replaced by "dumb." It may be "acting out" or poor judgment to drive while drunk, not immoral. An excuse for a crime or assault may be summed up in the statement "He asked for it." The excuse for not commenting on a tough issue used to be "it's controversial." Now a tough question is dodged

---

[*]"Mirage—Words that We Live By" (February 11, 1985).

by saying, "It is too complex for the short time at my disposal." The phrase "legally permissible" is often used to justify an essentially immoral act. Other words and phrases that are used to defend the attack or to confuse a moral issue include: "underprivileged," "disadvantaged," "window of opportunity," "straightening out priorities," "moral majority," "there are no quick fixes," "indepth study," "national security," "restructuring," and "hard choices." The real beauties are words that stand for emotions and attitudes.

As the international moral crisis deepens, old standby words are being readied like guided missiles to bring down political opponents. The governor of the State of New York, Mario Cuomo, seems to be in the vanguard of this trend. In his 1984 keynote address before the Democratic National Convention, he labeled his party the "caring" party, inferring that other parties did not care about the poor or the unemployed. Governor Cuomo addressed the newspaper publishers in San Francisco in May 1986. At this time he admonished the papers for not publicizing the unfortunates of our culture who were sacrificed to save the affluent. Columnist George Will, in commenting on the speech, dubbed Cuomo "Mr. Compassion," for intimating that those who did not stand up for compassion are morally defective.*

Compassion is not love, nor is it a moral principle. It is a combination of sympathy, concern, and projection of oneself into the unfortunate predicament of another. A feeling of compassion can stimulate a person to help another, but it is incapable of determining the moral quality of the act.

George Will has exposed a great deal of word magic. In the article mentioned above, he refers to a new word coined by Joseph Epstein, editor of the *American Scholar,* "virtuecrats." These are people of the Left and the Right who barrage us with political arguments based on pseudomorality. "I am holier than thou" will become "I am more virtuous than you." Righteous indignation may become the order of the day. Advancements in media technology have paralleled expansion in the use of word magic by public policy-making groups and political platform planners. So many words have too many meanings. This lack of word fidelity has always been exploited in controlling human behavior. It is beginning to appear that immorality on a worldwide basis increases in proportion to the expansion of communication technology and the numbers of people who are confused by a daily dose of news and opinions.

---

*"Mr. Compassion Makes a Speech," *San Francisco Chronicle* (May 9, 1986).

We must be on guard for everyday words that change a statement into a nonstatement or into a statement with doubtful meaning. Here are a few such words: "may," "can," "could," "ought," "possible," "probably," "never," "sometimes." An example: "Such a policy will raise your taxes." This is a definite and clearcut prediction. But with an ever so slight change, the speaker can plant fear of a tax increase in a listener's mind without making a prediction: "Such a policy may raise your taxes." The speaker might have easily used "can" or "could." This is the way people attempt to motivate voters without offering proof, or without risking the embarrassment of a failed prediction.

Many political policy-making groups in our society have strong socialist goals. They urge us to do a better job of distributing wealth, providing housing for the poor, job replacement, and training for the unemployed. Their means of emotionally motivating us are to point out the very real suffering of millions of our fellow citizens. However, they fail to present innovative, workable plans, detailed as to operations, administration, and sources of financing. Those individuals and groups who make sincere and earnest recommendations for the moral improvement of society must be encouraged to also tell us how to do it. We need a basis for determining their true motives: gaining political power, laying claim to our property, or genuinely helping the unfortunate.

We have a tendency to change the labels on things without changing the contents. Why do we call a jail or prison a rehabilitation center or a correctional facility? We have no verifiable evidence that we know how to rehabilitate or correct criminals. Why is public charity called social welfare, social endowment, or entitlements? Is there something especially moral about being entitled to public funds rather than simply being given public funds? We call warehouses for the incompetent aged rest homes. Mistakes in public agencies due to poorly coordinated staff work are called miscommunication rather than administrative failure. Misinformation replaces falsehood and lying. When it comes to children, we have reform schools, juvenile detention centers, houses of correction, penal institutions, youth authority facilities, all of which are for youthful offenders rather than juvenile law breakers, criminals, or incorrigibles. Our understanding of moral issues and the motivations behind social problems, governmental institutions, and political objectives is not particularly well served by the use of misleading and distractive word magic. It would be wise of us to cut out the verbal nonsense and use plain, simple, descriptive language. Ponder this: over the main entrance to the United States Supreme

Court building is the inscription "Equal Justice For All." Does that tell us what goes on in there?

4

Developing Moral Knowledge

The learning of morality in any culture is complex and varied. We can prove this to ourselves by remembering moral learning experiences drawn from our own childhood. Life teaches us that no two people have exactly the same moral upbringing. Our diverse society is made up of a conglomeration of ethnic, educational, occupational, religious, political, and socioeconomic levels, each contributing complexity and variation to moral learning experiences. Two other important factors complicate the teaching and learning of moral behavior: children vary according to age in capacity to comprehend and learn moral behaviors, and even children growing up in the same family are exposed to subtly different moral learning experiences than those of their siblings.

Teaching as well as learning morals will be touched on again and again as we proceed. A few of my own moral learning experiences and observations follow. Compare them, if you like, with your own personal experiences.

As a child I learned that morals have something to do with being good and it seemed that having fun had something to do with being bad. As kids my cohorts and I would do anything to avoid being called a goody-goody. Learning how to be good was not on our agenda. Somehow, without our knowing it, we learned from the example of our elders the basis of civilized behavior. We were not taught a code of neighborly conduct and acceptable social attitudes. We just found ourselves fitting in and it gave us confidence and a sense of belonging. I do not recall any formal instruction in morals during my elementary and secondary school years.

It was something we young people picked up here and there in real-life experience at home, in informal school situations, and in the community.

When I was a young man, people gave me the impression that they had little or nothing further to learn about morality. It was just something all of us picked up along the way and it was really quite simple, mainly just a bunch of rules and laws. Most people, even my parents, were reluctant to talk about morals. They acted as though this subject was a private matter not open to question. When I am with people today, fifty years later, I find little change. Folks can know each other for a long time and still avoid discussions of moral issues, religion, and politics. I have often thought that table games like bridge were invented so friends could sidestep serious, revealing discussions of personal matters. Older children and teenagers developed an aversion to being lectured on morals, personal conduct, and proper deportment and manners. Parents, teachers, and others who tackled this job were looked upon as killjoys. I have met few adults who show much interest in moral problems, yet they generally agree that human behavior is becoming more unreliable and dangerous.

During adolescence I met few adults who claimed to know the source of moral conventions. I was told that moral conduct was supposed to be taught in Sunday School and that everything we needed to learn about morals could be found in the Bible. The high school I attended had a curriculum rich in Latin, European languages, literature, mathematics, physics, chemistry, and arts and crafts, but anything resembling moral history or thought was absent. I recall teachers of history and literature occasionally leading discussions that bore directly on moral problems in historical and fictional plots and interpersonal events. This is as close as I came to receiving illumination on the importance and practicality of moral knowledge.

Probably everyone's personal history includes episodes where his or her conduct was found to be unacceptable or not to be tolerated. Such episodes usually come about dramatically and quickly as when we are caught in the act of doing something that is forbidden by law, or is harmful to ourselves or to others. I can remember several such episodes. One, in particular, jarred me from head to toe. It was a fast and lasting lesson in morality. I had teased my sister until she cried, and I was made aware that my father had witnessed this act when he came up to me and smartly slapped my face. In this critical instant I learned that tormenting my sister did not sit well with my father; that causing another to suffer can backfire; and that dominating a weaker person is not a constructive use of power.

I also realized my father's use of superior power did not derive from a desire to torment me but to protect my sister. From this event I learned what many years later I would call a moral principle, that the deliberate harming of others is immoral. During the personal episode described above, my father made no verbal remarks before or after the incident. I also learned that nonverbal learning can be potent.

I have mentioned that people have difficulty talking about morals because they confuse them with religious doctrines regarding sinfulness, or political opinions of the far Left or Right, or emotional reactions and social attitudes. Another thing that makes it extremely difficult to talk about morality is that the term is most readily understood when we talk about immorality. It is easy to draw up a list of words that exemplify immorality: e.g., "murder," "assault," "arson," "terrorism," "rape," "swindling," and so on, but it takes a lot of doing to define their opposites. We do not speak of the virtue of being nonmurderous or anti-incendiary. Morality is most easily but inaccurately described as the opposite of immorality.

An additional complicating factor that blocks intelligent discussion of morals is the notion that they are elastic and relative; that one person's morals are another's immorality. In matters of taste, one person's music may be another person's noise. Musical preferences are a matter of culture. If a person is brought up on a diet of classical music, a hard rock band performance may sound like noise, but this is all right. No harm is usually done. However, if a person is brought up without moral perspectives, he or she is potentially dangerous to society. It is difficult for people to seriously consider that morals are not relative, but are definite elements of human behavior that are identifiable, established, and have some of the qualities of natural laws. So, we cannot just say that random killing is acceptable to some but unacceptable to others. The very core of morality is objective and trans-social as well as transcultural. Notions of sin and certain rules and laws have shifted with location and historical time frame. Once it was forbidden to dance or play cards on Sundays. These religious prohibitions are no longer publicly observed. The prohibition of manufacturing or selling alcoholic beverages in the United States was repealed. Sin and laws can be repealed. Basic moral principles, however, cannot be repealed any more easily than the law of gravity. Parts Two and Three explain this concept in greater detail.

The world is at the crossroads of morality. We humans are going to continue to flounder in a murky brew of moral and legal ineptitude laced with assorted opinions and emotions stemming from every conceivable activity, prejudice, and system of policy and belief that can be imagined. Among the growing list of major problems we face are continuing religious and political wars, achieving nuclear disarmament, relieving worldwide economic stress, reducing or eliminating environmental pollution, eradicating crime, preventing the splintering of society into hostile power groups, governments confounded by insoluble problems and recalcitrant citizens, a cantankerous and impotent United Nations, and dilemmas raised by advances in technology. Everyone of these vexatious problems springs from moral failure, from moral ignorance, from immorality, amorality, and, sadly, from a lack of a rational, verifiable universally accepted body of moral principles. The United Nations declaration of basic human rights as set forth in the Helsinki accords falls far short of being a universal moral code.

It does not require special powers of observation to become aware that the world we live in is wonderful, inspiring, and exciting while at the same time gripped by horror, degeneration, and fear. Having been born in 1907, my life has spanned most of the twentieth century. I am reminded daily that I have lived in the best of times. Yet I witnessed two of the most destructive and unsettling world wars in history. The century began, however, with the rapid development of electrical energy distribution systems, electric light, mass production of automobiles, a network of railroads that crisscrossed the continent, the construction of the Panama Canal, the development of the telephone, the advent of motion pictures, and many other marvels. As a boy, I was cognizant of the contrasts of moral and immoral events, but I have no recollection of thinking there was anything unusual about my world. I was the offspring of a remarkable but messy century.

Despite the utopian promise of the scientific and technological explosion, we were regularly visited by economic problems and social unrest. During the Great Depression, I could look down from my apartment window in New York City and see people of all ages searching through garbage cans for a bite to eat. A short walk brought me to "Hooverville," a shanty town built on the banks of the Hudson River as a citizens' reminder of what President Hoover's economic policies had done to the nation. There I talked with fellow Americans who were hapless victims of the economic downfall. They had nothing favorable to say about their packing crate shacks or their skimpy meals, which occasionally featured rat stew. These trips to Hooverville were my first personal adventures in the morality maze and they affected me deeply. While this was going on, I was living well as a student at Columbia University.

The century swept on through economic recovery and World War II. Then came the fast-paced postwar period. No sooner had the United Nations been formed than the United States became a world police force, first supporting South Korea and then South Vietnam in two tragic wars for survival. Neither side won the Korean war. It ended as it began and as it remains, two belligerent Koreas. The Vietnam war ended in the defeat of the United States. These wars stand as memorials to the moral ineptitude and military miscalculations of world leaders and the abuse and waste of human resources.

Today, we find ourselves confronted on every side by worldwide social, economic, political, legal, and religious dilemmas that make all else in our history appear puny. Our leaders struggle with problems that not only get worse, but multiply. We remain in disarray, nonplussed, stymied, and looking for guidance that never arrives. Being bankrupt and unable to balance a budget, the United States has lost its main source of international power—money. Poverty, unemployment, political corruption, the business practices of large corporations, drug abuse, a failed educational system, street crime, and the dangers of nuclear proliferation stand in stark contrast to the "high-tech" revolution that promised a vastly improved quality of life and yet charts no new course to a moral world.

5

The Morality Maze

We cannot help but marvel at the genius, courage, togetherness, military might, and economic treasure that was assembled by the Western world in the wars of this century. One need only look at the extraordinary feats performed during the recent Gulf War to appreciate our military and technological capabilities. With all this remarkable ability how did we get into the present mess? Humankind has constructed a social, economic, and political environment for itself that is incomprehensibly immoral, dangerous, and emotionally disturbing. Despite it all, we have forged ahead with scientific and technological advances, more than doubling our knowledge every ten years. However, we do not have the same level of genius when it comes to using our hard-won knowledge as we do in acquiring it.

The trouble we are in is not adequately described by a mere recital of the breakdown of civilization. The fault lies largely in our failure to be as innovative in moral conceptualizations as in science and technology. Part of the fault is the way we were raised. We were not brought up to make the moral decisions necessary to improve our lot. We have been magnificent at putting down a few tyrants and their military machines, but have managed our victories like simpletons. Until quite recently, the United Nations had not fulfilled our expectations, but it is now on the way to revealing its potential for preserving world peace and security. It is not an exaggeration to say that we are in the midst of a critical juncture in history, a moral crisis. Governments cannot control their citizens, laws are not obeyed or enforced, and the world's religions are losing the power to inspire and lead. Government, the law, and religion can tell us what to do, but they cannot tell us how to do it. The roots of morality have become intertwined with social, economic, and political theories; with religious doctrines and emotional motivations; and with the perversion of every form of communication.

Newspaper headlines tell a gruesome story of the times we live in. Here are a few headlines taken at random from one large city paper over the course of just a few days.

"Religious Fighting Rages in Lebanon"

"Twenty-Eight Die in Beirut as Militias Battle with Artillery"

"Senate Panel's Grim Report on Nursing Homes"

"Teamster Chief, Aides, and FBI Agent Indicted"

"Paris Terrorists Attack Interpol Headquarters"

"Engineer Seized on Spy Charges"

"Baby Found in Car Trunk"

"Muni Official Named in Theft of Fares"

"Judge Gets 15 Years for Bribes in Chicago"

"AIDS Spread by Body Builders—Passing the Needle for Steroid Injections"

"Drunken Driving Arrests Top 1800"

"Ex-Atlantic City Mayor Sentenced"

"Murderer Seizes Jetliner"

"Kidnapped Diplomat Rescued"

"Polish Cop Admits He Clubbed Priest"

"Church to Fight in Courtroom"

"Waves of Bombing in Southern France"

"Indian Army on Alert After Sikhs Kill 13"

"Rebels Kill Relief Workers in Ethiopia"

We might imagine these headlines as drawn from the official publication of some kind of weird psychotic society. We read the same old stuff every day, yet we are not bored—horrified and bewildered, perhaps, but not bored.

A leading architect of the morality maze is government. It is government that attempts to translate our most basic moral principles, needs, and desires into law. Proposals for new laws and the elimination or modification of old ones are introduced to legislative bodies by politicians who are presumably representing some segment of their constituencies. All these well-meaning and possibly overworked lawmakers were put in their important positions by ordinary citizens like us; we must not expect them to be better or worse than we are. Be this as it may, we see no end to the public demand for new laws or the zeal with which lawmakers attempt to supply the demand. Regretfully, we have no real proof that all of these new laws have accomplished any useful purpose. To the contrary, they add to confusion about the primary moral objectives of a society. Laws passed one year are rescinded or struck down by a court the next. Some are forgotten. Some are unpopular, inconsequential, or unenforceable. A convincing example is the 1919 Volstead Act wherein Congress prohibited the sale of intoxicating liquors. It was repealed in 1933.

We are beginning to wonder if government itself can be trusted. This is a strong signal that society is in a crisis of government as well as morals. Is our government moral? In a democracy such as ours perhaps crises of government and morals are more alike than different. Can a society with serious moral problems expect to maintain, let alone establish, a moral government? Every facet of American life is declining in quality despite continued government aid (albeit in smaller increments) and new laws. Our national debt alone is proof that we cannot manage our fiscal affairs any better now than a hundred years ago. We are falling behind all Western-style democracies in literacy; training in the sciences; and in our efforts to reduce crime rates, drug abuse, and health-care costs. The list is a long one. Maybe the term *moral majority* should be replaced by *alienated majority,* meaning those who feel powerless in the face of big government, big religion, big business, and big international politics.

In trying to help people and give support to their diverse hopes and aspirations, government inadvertently aids and abets immorality. Public assistance programs provide good examples. It is morally inept to help people who can help themselves. Government has infantilized a large segment of the population through welfare, training large numbers of people from childhood to look toward government as a crazy mother who will give her all. Welfare cheaters are legion. We are well into the third generation of welfare mothers, dependents producing dependents. This adjunctive society is a world unto itself, organized and legally assisted to defend and capitalize on welfare entitlement programs. This is a new, nonproductive aristocracy of the poor who have a legal right to tax their government.

It would be tedious and perhaps nonproductive to protract this recital of socioeconomic problems brought on by government. A few examples other than welfare might jog our memories at this point, bringing our minds to bear on the seriousness of the moral blunders of government in the recent past. There is the post World War II inflation, which to this day is sponsored in large measure by Washington. It has been estimated that the loss of purchasing power of money earned and saved by Americans during the last half century has run into trillions of dollars. Congress was not oblivious to this condition when it kept increasing the national debt level. Is this an example of moral responsibility? Allowing a three trillion dollar national deficit to accumulate raises more than a question of morality; it poses a question of sanity itself. Occasionally Congress will pass an important bill that is certain to gain presidential approval. But to achieve a majority for passage, the Congress accepts an irrelevant amendment that is known to be inimical to the president. A moral president will veto the whole bill rather than sign into law a bad rider. This coupling of incongruent legislation is a form of blackmail and dishonesty, yet no Congress has had the moral courage to outlaw riders or to give the president a line item veto.

One last example: political candidates and platform writers make thousands of promises that have not been kept. A promise is a verbal contract between candidate and voter. Breaking a contract is immoral. Government should lead us out of the puzzling morality maze, not entangle us further.

6

Roadblocks to Moral Understanding

Government does not set the best example of morality for its citizens. I regard this as a serious roadblock to a moral society. Education is another: colleges and universities have offered courses in moral philosophy and ethics, yet they are not among the more popular courses. University schools of medicine, education, business management, and law are giving far more attention to the historical and theoretical basis of morals and ethics than ever before. A new professional specialty is developing: moral and ethical counseling. These specialists work with any organization that is suffering from moral problems such as sexual harassment; questionable business practices; minority rights violations; and proper treatment of clients, customers, and fellow workers. I was surprised recently to find that a university gave an unruly fraternity the choice of shutting down or accepting a course of training from a counseling ethicist. There is at least budding recognition that moral education cannot be left to chance.

The great problem of moral education is: *what to teach?* We have no recognized unified body of moral principles ready for incorporation into the school curriculum. Plenty of textbooks, materials, and audio visual aids are available on almost every subject under the sun, but not in the field of morals. A few capable resource people are visible in public school moral education, but not many. The schools have depended on the home, the family, and the church or synagogue to teach morals. All have failed to a marked degree.

Social scientists have been great at spotting moral flaws in society but they have not done very well at developing solutions. The question of how people are motivated to follow moral principles has baffled psychologists. The difficulties arise from the complexity of human nature and the heterogeneous composition of American society today. So many things have an influence on the shaping of moral concepts, on their acceptance, and their observance through human behavior. Students in this area must consider biological factors such as heredity, hormonal and other biochemical influences, nutritional variations, diseases, and drug abuse, to mention a few. Racial and ethnic interactions, religious and educational variables, and, of course, psychosocial competence are factors also in the adjustment of human behavior as we use and misuse moral principles.

The law is the great champion of morality in our society, but it's erecting roadblocks to moral behavior. In homogeneous, less sophisticated societies, conventions that embody customs and morals are the guides for conduct. As a society matures, the state, through its legal apparatus, takes on the role of codifying our most basic moral attitudes. Conventions, passed down from one generation to another, wither away as the law multiplies its moral prerogatives. Conventional morality is ultimately pushed aside by legal codes, rules, regulations, and penalties. A paternalistic relationship develops between citizens and their government. This inverse relation between conventions and laws leads to moral disintegration. In a modern society marital and family law requires an extensive written penal code, while in earlier times a simple set of customs and traditions sufficed.

People foresake as many responsibilities as possible, pushing them off on government and the courts. This movement, if it can be called that, is not aimed at creating or accepting an authoritarian government, but serves as a convenient escape from personal responsibility. Moral persons want to assume as much responsibility for themselves as possible. It is the job of government to help them do this. At this time in history the legal arm of government is caught up in the same moral confusion as the society it is struggling to serve. I have argued in this paragraph that the law is not clarifying moral issues. The popular television program "The People's Court" has done as much to educate ordinary citizens in the nature, function, and processes of law as any other educational agency in our society. And, it has taken care to illustrate the relationship of behavior to law and morality.

Since World War II, we have seen an increase in religious cults, advocates of alternate lifestyles, anti-establishment communes, dozens of lay therapies for body and mind, devil worship, witchcraft, astrology, mind reading and fortune telling, investigation of past lives, channeling, unscientific applications of quantum mechanics to psychic phenomena, oriental metaphysical theories, and methods of tapping hidden energy sources within the self. The list could go on and on. These "new age" movements have been accompanied by sophisticated science fiction movies and television dramas, and by a precipitous drop in the popular interest in science.

The rise of mysticism; the decline of enthusiasm for science among the general population; the lowered respect for government; the apparent flourishing of Christian fundamentalism; the growth in professional sports, mass entertainment, and drug abuse; and the malaise of our public schools combine to form a baffling mix. None of this augers well for conquering the morality maze. It seems to be getting more befuddling and tortuous. This predicament is further proof that we are in the center of upheaval. And more roadblocks appear daily. One of the more noticeable factors is the splintering of society into innumerable special-interest groups. Our oldest established institutions are being stressed to the breaking point: governments everywhere are on trial along with education, religion, and the administration of law. We are moving toward change, perhaps toward new conceptualizations of our major institutions, if not of civilization itself.

A little-noticed roadblock to thinking, expanding moral knowledge, or just becoming more aware of our own problems as a society, is the constant and growing demands on our time. I am not referring to time spent on earning a living, but on things like commuting; waiting in checkout lines; maintaining the machines we buy to do our work; paperwork at home for insurance, banking, income taxes; garden and household chores; and the like. If we have any leisure time, there are plenty of diversions and distractions to use it up: entertainment, sports, travel, television, motion pictures, and music. These can sop up all the spare time of our existence, using as much time as our primitive ancestors used in food gathering, and it is doubtful that we are better off for it. The media tends to make us passive observers rather than active participants. We have given up important options to manage and control ourselves. We have been weakened rather than strengthened, and wooed into a neglectful proprietorship of the self.

It behooves everyone to learn the facts of morality. We cannot turn away from moral claims and counterclaims that will occupy the thinking and politics of America and the world during the ensuing decade and on into the new century. People in the public eye are going to be appraised on the basis of their moral stature and knowledge as much or more so than on their qualifications in law, business, industry, science, and the other advanced accomplishments of civilization. The trouble ahead lies in the world of morals and jurisprudence.

This is a good time to explore the meaning of morality: its origins, development, present status, and uses in everyday life. Armed with moral knowledge we can be our own best judges of dogmas, doctrines, customs, manners, and opinions. Better yet, we can conduct our relations with family, neighbors, and fellow workers with confidence and satisfaction. In reading this book a lot of unfamiliar ideas will be coming your way. Be a quiet skeptic with an open mind, and enjoy yourself.

Part Two
Morality: Its Origin and Development

7

In the Beginning

The origins of morality go back to the beginnings of human experience. We would not be here today but for the fact that our primitive forebears took care of their offspring. Caring for or about something is a basic moral principle that has been around since the beginning. We may call caring for offspring instinctual or a genetic survival mechanism, but regardless of how we label parenting, it is a requirement of nature for all living creatures.

I believe that the moral behavior of caring, which, of course, includes protecting, is as essential for humankind's survival as it is for any living entity. In this perspective, morals appear as a natural phenomenon in the same sense as gravity or electrical energy. Other moral elements grew with human experience, perhaps as mere products of trial and accidental success, stumbled onto like most great discoveries. It is important at the onset to note that moral discoveries and practices were essential to the survival of humankind, as much so as fang, food, and procreation.

The taproot of morality is necessity. The human repertoire of moral elements grew unevenly over eons. A review of moral history reveals, here and there, surges and lapses of moral innovation, conservation, and practice. Since the beginning of history, records show that all cultures rise and fall. Anthropologists have been successful in showing the beginnings, the development, and the eventual decay of prehistoric people and their cultures. This phenomenon involves many components, but one that is found in all failed societies, to some degree, is a failure to follow basic, necessary moral elements. Necessity is not just the mother of invention but the mother of morals.

A teaching device used by many before me is a bit of fiction about the moral predicament of one lone person on Earth. For a moment suppose you are the only person on Earth. Survival itself would be practically impossible, but you would not have to be concerned with the moral appraisal of interpersonal relations or with conduct—both of which are operational factors in morality—because they never existed.

Being the only person, you would not have to worry about being mugged, murdered, raped, kidnapped, held hostage, or enslaved. Instead of being concerned with assassins and terrorists, you would have to be on the lookout for other dangerous animals. Furthermore, you could not commit an immoral act, you could do no wrong, you could not even be sinful.

Problems of law and order, political intrigue, conspiracy, betrayal, graft, dishonesty, lying, fraud, robbery, incendiarism, child molestation, drunk driving, environmental pollution, medical dilemmas, nuclear war or any other kind of war would not be on your daily bill of fare. There would be no reason for concern with respect to concepts of right and wrong, good and evil, sin and absolution, morality and immorality, justice and injustice, ethical and unethical, and the matter of freedom and civilization. All such concepts would not exist, and even if they were introduced, they would have no meaning.

You would be totally free. You would have two major choices: to live or die. If you wanted to live, you alone could assert this right and carry it out as best you could. Your own body would be the only property with which you would have to be concerned. Its needs and demands would have to be met if you wished to live. No one else would be around to help you take care of your most valuable possession or property, your own living body. You would be the sole proprietor of your being. The organism that you are came to you from nature. Under the circumstances, you may not receive much joy or benefit from this gift. The pains and burdens of a solitary existence could be eliminated by self-destruction. This could be accomplished without having to worry about your immortal soul or about harming anyone else. As the sole inhabitant of Earth, you would be properly described as *amoral*: ignorant of and therefore not concerned with what we call morals.

The foregoing fictional account of a solitary person on Earth illustrates that a population of one is intrinsically amoral. Such a person, by definition, could be neither moral nor immoral.

But suppose that one other person, male or female, comes into your life. It would be possible to expect to have an improved existence. You would now have the prospect of companionship, someone to help you with food gathering, someone to protect you while you slept. You and the "other" might find many ways to take care of each other. Communication of some sort would inevitably develop. Life could conceivably become more bearable.

This picture of two interacting and, to some extent, cooperative inhabitants might soon be marred. Fighting over food, the division of labor, where to migrate, and other serious matters could soon dim life's bright prospect. This duo would find it hard to survive as a unit without a few rules of conduct. Which person does what, and when, might be an important place to start, like learning to take turns at regular chores, caring for and using each other's possessions, such as they might be, and, of course, protecting each other. These rules of conduct would grow out of necessity. They would, in all likelihood, be almost childishly simple. The test for such rules of conduct would be their workability. If they helped in the attainment of biological essentials, they stood a good chance of enduring; if not, they would be abandoned. We might think of this situation as the very beginnings of moral order, law, and government.

As likely as not, one of the two individuals would attempt to dominate the other. This might become the first master and slave, or battered wife situation, or an elementary form of dictatorship. What could have been the birth of morality would be nipped in the bud. Of course, the submissive partner might rise up in a fit of rage and slay the dictator, setting a precedent for the assassination of leaders that has punctuated the whole of human history. While it is easy to imagine early human existence as shot through and through by strife, quarreling, and power struggles, a modicum of tranquility and cooperation had to exist or our species would not be here today.

Now let us add a few more people to our fictional illustration, say a dozen or so, to make up a small band or tribe. This revised situation might encourage us to picture an immediate improvement in food supplies, environmental management, mutual-protection techniques, and the value people place on others. We might witness some civil behavior, some showing of gratitude, some caring for a wounded member of the tribe, some glimmering of love and good will. Also, we can picture a tough, demanding life, a scarcity of food, cruel weather, and other hardships too numerous to mention. We can only guess at what would happen to emerging moral behavior patterns under conditions of great adversity.

In modern times, when a society is disintegrating, the moral and legal regulation of interpersonal relations and their enforcement deteriorate or temporarily disappear. During periods of social unrest, vandalism, looting, robbery, hijacking goods in transit, murder, rape, and forsaking discipline and decency are common if not inevitable. The barbarians seem unstoppable and bent on running a course to meaningless exhaustion. Fortunately, however, exceptions do occur. Great Britain, an advanced, stable society that for years suffered tremendously crushing blows at home and abroad during World War II, failed to collapse internally. To the contrary, high levels of moral valor and discipline were sustained throughout the war. It is only rational to suppose that some primitive peoples were likewise able to surmount great odds while others, in different circumstances, succumbed to demoralization, panic, and defeat.

Primitive humans, like their modern counterparts, experimented with strategies designed to control the behavior of others. Some individuals may have employed threats of harm, beating adversaries into submission, or even killing them if they refused to comply. Others may have experimented with less violent means of control: offering a gift for compliance, reasoning with their adversaries, or making a contract to give help in exchange for help. To some degree, all of these strategies may have worked in getting people to comply with the desires of others, but some were costly to tribal or familial strength and survival ability. Fights to the death between hunters would almost immediately diminish the food supply, to say nothing of weakening the defense capability of the tribe against predatory animals and dangerous bands of migrating humans.

8

Moral Development among Primitives

Speculating about the development of morals among primitives resembles fiction. Anthropologists and paleontologists have arduously searched for and painstakingly unearthed the skeletal remains and artifacts of primitive humanoids. We know that humans have been around for millions of years. Possibly hundreds of humanoid types have come and gone. Evidence indicates that humankind, as known today, existed as prototypes fifty thousand years ago. We have no way to ascertain anything whatsoever about their moral development. Perforated skulls have been found with a single stone inside, suggesting that the original owner had been killed by a stone-tipped weapon of some kind. This does not tell us, however, whether the victim was killed in battle or ambushed by a murderer. Among primitive societies a few, at least, must have lived in peace and harmony for centuries, indicating the employment of some kind of a conventional code of conduct.

Moral principles and behavior are outgrowths of biological necessity, their primary component of morality. It is easy to see this in the case of caring. Obviously, caring supports biological needs. This is true of food gathering, defending oneself, protecting others, prohibiting murder, legitimizing sexual unions, and training children in survival techniques, to mention a few. It is not so easy at first to see how planning a migration, truthfulness, keeping promises (verbal contracts), friendliness, and a desire to help are moral components of the human being that have as their foundation biological necessity. Yet these are all behaviors that promote the well-being of the community and strengthen the physical and mental capacities of the group, thus enhancing the survival prospects of the members. Moral elements can be arranged in a rank order from immediate needs to remote needs: when the concept of self-defense is at issue it is a now-or-never event, unlike a proposed migration, which may be months away. In self-defense we may have no choice but to act now. In planning a migration, the safety of all concerned is a major consideration. The migratory journey is necessary for desirable climatic change and improved food supply.

All moral elements mentioned to this point are biologically derived; none is arbitrary, capricious, or relative. Omit any one and the survival potential of the tribe is diminished to a greater or lesser extent. No further extension of the foregoing speculative descriptions of the moral development of prehistoric humans will be attempted. We can now turn to explorers and anthropologists of recent times who have discovered and lived with primitive peoples, studying their moral behavior firsthand. One of their important findings is that determinants of acceptable and unacceptable behavior are outgrowths of attaining certain biological necessities in the context of a specific ecosystem. This helps account for the dramatic differences between cultures. Two brief examples may help to illustrate my point.

Arctic explorers were amazed to find that an Eskimo man would invite a strange male visitor to sleep with his wife. If the invitation was accepted, both the Eskimo man and wife were pleased. If refused, however, the Eskimos were likely to feel rebuffed or insulted. The pristine Eskimo ecosystem placed no taboo on extraspousal sex. It was not a family or population threat and complicating sexual factors such as venereal disease did not exist. Also, in the sparse and scattered Eskimo population, the sharing of warmth, love, and companionship was likely to have been a biological advantage during the cold, dark, lonely Arctic winters.

Eskimos had no reason to steal from each other: borrowing property without special permission was allowed, particularly hunting and fishing implements. A stranger, far from home, might take hunting equipment from an unfamiliar Eskimo encampment. It was customary, however, to return such private property promptly after use. Hunting and fishing equipment were vital to survival. This is an example of a moral element or principle: the implied permission to have access to common survival necessities.

Another such element might be found in the following: On long marches during winter, a band of Eskimos could not carry or support a handicapped or severely injured person, particularly if the individual were elderly. Such an individual would be left behind, perhaps at a campsite, and allowed to freeze to death. This act was carried out in situations of dire necessity and accepted by both the elderly and their relatives. Under the circumstances this was a moral act grounded on the need to protect the survival chances of the whole band.

In her book *Coming of Age in Samoa*, anthropologist Margaret Mead tells of living among primitive Polynesians.* She found customs and conventions that were strange to Americans. When, for example, children were old enough to take an active interest in sex they were free to experiment. If a girl got pregnant, her elders were accepting of the event. Babies became part of the tribe and all adults treated all children as though they were their own. Men and women paired off on a preferential basis. They were free to break up such a relationship and form another, or remain single. They had no institution of marriage as we know it, no code of marital conduct that applied to all couples, and no rule of sexual fidelity, though fidelity was observed by some couples. Mead paid close attention to the stability of couples who lived together. Much to her surprise, she discovered that the Polynesian couples had more lasting and harmonious relationships than comparable married couples in the United States.

We learn from such observational studies of primitive peoples that their small-scale societies are at once strikingly similar and diverse. They are similar in that they create major moral guidelines for interpersonal and group conduct, the basic goal of which is survival. They are diverse in that they carry out their survival practices in quite different environmental situations. The problems of survival for Eskimos were vastly different than those of native Polynesians. These peoples practiced morality consistent with the demands of their unique ecosystem. If brought together, they would no doubt experience difficulties understanding one another's social customs, yet each might well appreciate the survival strategies of the other. From the foregoing we observe that moral behavior is a function of the total workings of a society and that it makes possible the attainment of biologically essential objectives. On the other hand, immoral behavior is any behavior that is inimical to the welfare of a society and its members.

---

*Copyright 1928 by Margaret Mead. (New York: William Morrow and Company, 1975), see especially pages 105–108, 201.

9

The Role of Religion and Government in the History of Morals

Our earliest records of the morals and laws of ancient civilizations had to wait for the invention of writing. Written history began approximately 6,000 years ago. The first fully developed code of laws, those of Hammurabi (who reigned from 1792 to 1750 B.C.) were unearthed at Susa, Persia (or what is now Iran) in 1902. Hammurabi described himself as a conqueror and lawgiver, and a real father to the people. He brought together the warring states of the lower Mesopotamian Valley and founded Babylon, the greatest city of his time. While a secular person, Hammurabi claimed his laws were approved by the gods. From these laws we gain a clear impression of the moral concerns and beliefs of Hammurabi's time.

In my opinion, the laws of Hammurabi, now known to have been based on Sumerian* prototypes, are more extensive in variety and scope than any other body of laws attributable to the ancient world. In fact, they can be compared favorably to our own laws, except that associated punishments were barbarous by our standards. Hammurabi left us 282 laws.† They were arranged under the following headings: Personal Property, Real Estate, Trade and Business, Family Law, Injuries, and Labor. Some of the specific laws deal with such topics as libel, theft, receiving stolen goods, looting, murder, bodily injury, treatment of slaves, family

---

*The inhabitants of Sumer lived in lower Babylonia from about 4000–1800 B.C.

†"Code of Hammurabi" as cited in *Encyclopedia Americana*, 1991 edition, volume 13, p. 750.

laws (covering offspring, divorce and inheritance) and the corrupt administration of justice. Many of the laws are surprisingly modern. For instance, if the state failed in its responsibility to protect the people, it was required to compensate victims of crimes. Also, the state saw to it that "justice" was done to orphans and widows. We are now getting around to this sort of law in the last quarter of the twentieth century.

The laws of Moses (the Mosaic law) are set forth as coming directly from God. These laws, seemingly patterned after those of Hammurabi, came after the Babylonian subjugation of the Jews. The first five books of the Old Testament of the Bible are the principal reference sources for the laws of Moses, particularly the Book of Leviticus. The Old Testament covers the period from 1200 B.C. to 200 B.C. No written records exist until after 200 B.C., and they are reconstructions of recollections of lost writings passed down for generations by word of mouth. In Exodus, following the Ten Commandments, a detailed recital of the laws of Moses adds little to our knowledge of morality in the ancient world beyond that provided by Hammurabi. This statement must not be construed as a judgment on the body of religious doctrine and wisdom contained in the Old Testament.

Here in Part Two I am focusing on the various forces that have shaped the development of moral concepts. When we contemplate the laws of Hammurabi and the Mosaic Code, we cannot help being awed by the huge amount of time, effort, experience, and thought that must have gone into bringing them to fruition. The laws of Hammurabi did not spring full blown from the mind of a single enlightened genius. Undoubtedly, these laws were based on moral principles that were countless centuries in the making and for which no written records exist.

Also, we may begin to question the opinion that religion is the fount of morality. Both religion and government are important in the history of moral development, not necessarily for generating morals but for preserving moral knowledge, for teaching it, and for using it to regulate and harmonize human behavior. Moral principles have been used by both religion and government as a rationale for, and as a means of, gaining social control over citizens and their institutions, presumably for the citizens' own benefit.

Morality begins with the interactions of people as they go about the daily work of survival and in so doing discover effective techniques for satisfying their biological needs and supplying advantages and life enhancers. As time-proven behavioral formulas emerged in association with the evolutionary development of concern for others, such as communal cooperation, mutual protection, friendly caring, keeping agreements, respecting each other's families and belongings, and carrying one's own burdens, these moral behaviors became customs—a body of common rules of conduct. When a society generally accepts and practices a body of customs and rules of conduct, it has achieved a level of culture that some will consider worthy of preserving, extending, refining, and passing on to future generations and to neighboring cultures. One of the first tasks in this preservation process is to teach morals, a responsibility most likely assumed by families, neighbors, friends, the medicine men, shaman, respected elders, and tribal or community leaders. Later, a more forceful role in the propagation of moral principles came with the rise of such socially powerful institutions as organized and formal religion, government, and education.

In the Judeo-Christian tradition, religious doctrines and moral principles are believed to have been derived from supernatural sources. The Ten Commandments, a moral code, are set forth in the Old Testament of the Bible (Exodus 20) as the revealed word of God. Today, it would be difficult to defend the first five commandments on moral grounds alone. They deal with what has become doctrinal religious rules such as worshipping but one true God; rejecting representations of God ("carved images") and the misuse of God's name; and honoring one's mother and father. The last five commandments—prohibiting murder, adultery, stealing, bearing false witness, or coveting a neighbor's property—would find acceptance today as moral principles, quite apart from religious considerations. Further, the last five commandments could have been derived from the laws of Hammurabi, which appeared hundreds of years before the Ten Commandments were received by Moses.

I should like to comment briefly on the fifth and tenth commandments. Concerning the fifth commandment, to honor one's mother and father, one wonders if people are really bound by principle to honor a mother and/or father who abused or deserted them? I think not. However, I know some individuals who vehemently defend this commandment under all circumstances. Also, the tenth commandment, against coveting a neighbor's wife or property, can be questioned as a moral principle, since envy and ardent desire hurt no one but the person who covets, unless they are acted out against others. The counterargument is that covetousness is an unhealthy state of mind and a needless suffering perpetrated on the self and, perhaps, indirectly on others and therefore can be classified as immoral. (The complex distinctions between *moral* and *immoral* are covered fully in Part Three.)

Occasionally, individuals and communities must decide which actions are most appropriate for their well-being. This is difficult to do where large numbers of people are involved. Such predicaments invite the formation of centralized social mechanisms that could specialize in organizing and managing a community. This need for a societal nerve center provided the medium for the evolution of both organized religion and formal government structures. Collectively, they could supply some of the ingredients of public decision making, such as information, records of past experience, essential moral directives, incentives, rules of propriety, and, perhaps, some wisdom and inspiration. In varying ways and degrees, both religion and government have served community needs, sometimes as allies, sometimes as opponents, and not infrequently they have functioned as a single organization rather than as separate institutions. The latter is seemingly true in the story of the ancient Jews, as told in the Old Testament.

One of the greatest progressive strides for humanity was the creation of government, which is itself a moral finding that has had an essential role in the evolution of civilization. Some form of government, however loose and unstructured it may be, is necessary for the most meager fulfillment of human biological requisites. Government is the foundation of an orderly society, its main function being the protection of its citizens and their property. It is quite possible that this should be the only function of government.

As an example of the moral regulative service provided by government, we need only consider for a moment the lowly automobile traffic signals. Without them, safety on the road would vanish and chaos would reign. A society without government would suffer a worse fate than auto traffic without signal lights. Whether or not we like it, government shapes the fundamental moral tone of society. It helps to hold the web of our destiny together for better or worse. Perhaps the discovery of government is one of the greatest of scientific findings, being a specific moral entity rather than just a mechanism for regulating the behavior of the body politic. The moral potential of government may fail, but only when its basic protective purpose is ignored or supplanted with other objectives.

Governmental administrators always should be conscious that the organization they are attempting to operate is one of humanity's principal moral instruments. Hammurabi claimed that his city, Babylon, was the great preserver and practitioner of moral law; however, after his lifetime the city faded and passed into oblivion. Thousands of governments have followed this course. Yet, enough continuity of government and public allegiance to moral customs has protected the human race from complete destruction. It seems that the powers of civilization have just barely maintained a slender lead over the forces of barbarism. The only way a government can maintain continuity is by protecting its citizens and their property. This is its moral imperative.

Throughout history governments have undertaken ambitious projects that have not been motivated by the moral function of protecting citizens and their property. This is especially true after the emergence of politically organized societies called *states*. Both states and smaller societies have waged predatory war on neighboring, even distant, peoples. The lust for territorial control, aggrandizement, riches, slaves, and other booty by power-hungry governments is a violation of their moral imperative and leads inevitably to human tragedy and, if carried too far, to the dissolution of governments.

Offensive, predatory warfare is a clear example of how the aims of states and their governments are placed above the welfare of ordinary citizens. Of course, many other examples demonstrate the theory that ordinary citizens exist to serve the state, a view which is at odds with the opposite theory that the state exists to serve its citizens by upholding what I have termed the moral imperative of government. States frequently behave like imperious individuals and regard their objectives as superior to those of their citizens. Thus, a state may exercise the right to redistribute the wealth of its citizens by taxation, confiscation, or outright plunder, or to give the property of its citizens to, say, foreign countries without first obtaining the specific consent of its own people.

The moral functions of government must of necessity be limited to the formulation of laws designed to protect the persons and property of its citizens; to the creation and employment of powers to enforce the laws of the land; to the operation of courts of law; to the imprisonment, fining, and, in some cases, banishment of law breakers; and to the maintenance of a system of national defense. Of course, the property-protection functions of today's governments would include our commonly owned and shared natural environment: outer space, the atmosphere, the oceans, water supplies, and other natural resources essential to survival.

It is hard to imagine a time when people did not wonder about metaphysical issues: the mysteries of life; how the world and life came to be; the purpose of it all; the question of a spirit or soul; the matter of life after death; why we suffer so much; and dozens of other questions that, to this day, remain in need of complete and final answers. In addition, people must have been open to help with all kinds of problems of living. It seems quite likely that religion was invented, at least partially, to satisfy these demands in addition to addressing the metaphysical questions. History reveals the emergence of many religions, each attempting, without much factual information, to explain metaphysical questions and inquiries focused on social behavior, moral issues, and our probable destiny under different proposals for social control.

All religions of which we are aware, both ancient and modern, have taken doctrinal positions on the mysteries of creation, of human life, of our duties to our fellow humans and to the supernatural generative power(s) that made and rule the world. It is clear that under these authoritarian views religions could direct and regulate acceptable conduct and discourage misbehavior. This leads me to argue that religion is a governing force, a form of government that sometimes assumes a transcendental posture.

I lean toward the opinion that moral laws were among the earliest discoveries of humankind and, as noted earlier, were absolutely necessary to our survival. Institutionalized religion moved beyond moral law to reveal universal theories of creation, and to postulate a world beyond ours peopled with humanlike gods, a supernatural spirit world, or godhead in which we are duty bound to believe, worship, placate, and obey. In some instances morals were described as the word of God, thus gaining in prestige and authority. One duty of believers was to live their lives according to explicit God-given rules of conduct. Failure to do so was regarded as sinful or immoral. Flagrant infractions of doctrinal rules could lead to severe punishment, such as being denied eternal life or entry to paradise.

In summary, religion and government made their historical debut together. Originally, they may have been one and the same thing. In any event, they performed overlapping functions. As populous cities came into existence, secular government became a separate institution retaining some ties to religion. Government, however, became the principal law maker and enforcer. Religion and government have existed side by side for thousands of years. They have advocated and advanced morality. However, when expedient, they have violated every moral principle, thus undermining the basic protective functions of government, which have never been totally effective.

We have no proof that religion or government originated moral principles. However, it is correct to say that religion preserved and taught these principles. It also is correct to say that government put them to use as the foundations of law. Most importantly, government, being itself a moral imperative, occupies the unique position of being essential not only to human existence but to the attainment of civilization. A community can conceivably survive without religion, but not without some kind of government. This concludes, for the time being, my analysis of the interactions of religion, government, and moral knowledge.

10

Human Nature as a Shaper of Morals

We humans are so constituted that what we need is linked to powerful biological drives. The need for nutrition is linked to hunger, the need for water to thirst, the need for warmth to being cold, the need for rest to fatigue, and so on. We have no choice but to acquire the necessities of life. Our lives are dominated by necessity. Today, we have all the needs of primitive peoples and must fulfill them in an ever more complex environmental setting. We work out of necessity and we seek employment in order to obtain the money with which to buy the food, clothing, and shelter we require to sustain ourselves. We brush our teeth, bathe, wear clothes, drive our cars safely, create huge systems of national defense, provide for the underprivileged and do dozens of other individual and group chores and social duties, if not out of dire necessity, at least for reasons crucial to survival, safety, and comfort.

In meeting our needs we pay in many ways. Individuals and society must provide various ever-changing forms of protection, which consume energy and wealth. The underlying fear of victimization by criminal assault undermines general health. Further, the aftermath of crime follows when its victims as well as their kin and neighbors suffer anguish and other debilitating or disruptive emotions. Harm to the bodies and possessions of victims is a heavy burden to those who suffer and to the social group of which they are a part. It is easy to understand immorality as doing harm to the bodies and lives of others. In contrast to immorality, morality is, and must always have been, a prized form of behavior throughout history.

The human body is equipped with immune systems that are on the job day and night defending us against infectious diseases, foreign substances, even cancer cells. Just as the basic physiology of our bodies possesses specialized immunological defenses against environmental threats and dangers, so the whole organism, including the brain (the organ of the mind), is equipped with the capacity to cope with various kinds of external threats and dangers. Our senses alert us to danger. We can fight or flee from a predator. We can protect our young. We can learn and remember for ready use a vast repertoire of defensive techniques that can be called upon over and over, added to, and perfected. All of the lore and history of coping with the exigencies of life can be handed down from generation to generation. This represents, in part, what we call convention and culture, and among the most important attributes of culture are the moral elements that steer interpersonal relations and lubricate the machinery of successful group activities. These moral elements are to the totality of a culture what the system of biological defenses are to the survival capability of individual human organisms: a kind of immune or protective system that undergirds culture and civilization.

The vitality and creativeness of a society are in no small measure determined by the quality of nutrition available. Mental capacity as well as purely physical strength and energy are dependent to a marked degree on food and the benefits of proper nutrition. This is most dramatically demonstrated in starving populations whose members quickly become helpless if more fortunate people do not intervene. Historical records show that in the early stages of large-scale starvation many moral prohibitions become useless and are abandoned. Lethargy ensues, then weakness and death. Short of starvation, advanced malnutrition is common and almost as insidious. Some nutrition authorities believe that a majority of Americans are malnourished even though they have the most abundant food supply in the world. We may think that the quality of diet and food supply should correlate positively, but they do not. Even today diseases linked to vitamin deficiency are not uncommon. The earliest signs of malnutrition consist of a dimming of mental alertness and the loss of social effectiveness, self-control, and reliability.

A growing body of evidence indicates that a wide variety of psychological problems is the result of vitamin deficiencies. People who lack adequate amounts of Vitamin B12, for example, may experience serious behavior changes before anemia develops. We have no way of knowing how many people in the world suffer diet-related mental handicaps that may affect their intellectual ability as well as moral behavior. Nutritional deficiencies have undoubtedly played an important role in the slowing the development of constructive moral behavior, a situation that still plagues the human race.

It will not be necessary here to more than mention the undermining of moral behavior that has increased with the growing popularity of recreational drug use. It has been estimated that 40 percent of the American population used recreational drugs in 1985. The percent would be higher if we included alcohol in the category of drugs. Top management in big business, finance, and government is alarmed over the increased drug use by their employees. The use of drugs is linked to declining worker productivity, reduced quality of work, absenteeism, and immoral conduct. I would be interested to know how addictive substances used through the ages have affected our moral development, but we have no statistics that reach back more than a few decades.

More than one in ten people in the United States will reveal a need for or seek professional treatment for serious behavior problems ranging from complete ego collapse to inappropriate and sometimes violent social behavior. I am not referring to people who necessarily need hospitalization or psychiatric treatment. I am alluding to large numbers of intelligent, even gifted individuals who are too mentally unbalanced to occupy the responsible leadership roles they play in government, business, education, and parenting. It was once estimated by the American Psychiatric Association that one in four persons are sociopathic: these people know little about and care even less for the mores of society. While driving a car, it is a little scary to realize that one out of every four drivers on the street could be a sociopathic character who rejects the rules and laws of the road in favor of self-made rules that show a regard only for his own hide and pleasure. How do sociopaths, drug addicts, congenital defectives, victims of diminished capacity, and the mentally unstable shape the moral quality of civilization? There are few answers to this intriguing question.

Unless catastrophe interferes, each generation of humans inherits the culture of the preceding generation. It also inherits certain genetic characteristics. How much of what we term moral behavior is actually passed down via genes and chromosomes? While we do not know the whole answer to this question, a number of psychosocial studies has been reported in the last few years indicating that some desirable and some undesirable behaviors may well be inherited.

11

Genetic Factors in the Roots of Morality

What will happen when we can prove conclusively that morality and behavior in general have specific and verifiable origins in genetics; that moral tendencies are not only formed by environment but by heredity? Plato and other ancient Greek philosophers argued about how much of human behavior was inborn and how much resulted from training and education in the home and the community. This has come to be known as the nature-nurture controversy.

When I was an undergraduate in college, I was told by socialistically oriented professors that crime, poverty, unemployment and other social ills were the result of environmental factors, such as free enterprise, capitalism, and individualism. I more or less accepted the notion that the goods of this world should be more equitably divided, that profits should be regulated, that labor unions should share in management, and so on. It was argued that if these and other measures were taken, then crime would disappear and poverty and unemployment would be things of the past.

In 1934, I found myself in the minority when I suggested that crime was the result of unfavorable environment. Men of my father's generation, if they had strong opinions concerning the cause of crime, invariably said criminals were born, not made. Needless to say, nurture ultimately won out over nature. Fifty years later the nature-nurture controversy is reasserting itself once more in the public mind. Today, we recognize and admit that programs designed to change the social environment have failed. The Great Society of President Johnson hasn't worked. Extensive social programs coupled with massive defense spending have brought the country to the brink of bankruptcy. Though billions have been spent on criminal rehabilitation programs, we have no solid evidence of success. Public education has not improved the lot of students despite ever-increasing costs. Now, we are beginning to hear again of scientific research indicating that antisocial and criminal behavior may be rooted in our genes.

A common immorality today is the drunk automobile driver. In the United States alone, drunk drivers kill more people annually than terrorists do world-wide. Clearly, drunk driving is as serious a moral failure as a rooftop sniper. What makes this example of immorality poignant is the recent discovery by researchers that troublesome genes are the major contributing factor in alcoholism.* It will soon be possible to search for offending genes in school children, 30 to 40 million of whom may have this inherited defect. Children who are found to have the defect can be given preventive education and therapy before drinking patterns are established. This may have a more profound affect on responsible driving than tough laws and sentences for convicted drunk drivers.

A widely popularized biological finding that has been around quite a few years is that males born with an extra Y chromosome are apt to be violently aggressive and dangerous. An accompanying theory is that this hereditary factor can and possibly should be counteracted by identifying boys possessing an extra Y chromosome and giving them special socioemotional therapy or education during their elementary school years.† A number of articles and books reporting studies of the degree to which criminal behavior is inherited have appeared in the 1980s. The authors are convinced that their research gives weight to the common opinion that criminal behavior is inherited: not just a propensity to murder, but strong leanings toward a variety of serious crimes.

Since World War II, an increasing number of scientific studies of the genetics of antisocial behavior have taken place. It has been a slow and difficult process, usually requiring studies of twins, both fraternal and identical. Findings show that identical twins are about twice as likely as fraternal twins to demonstrate a similar propensity toward criminal activity. An extensive study by Karl O. Christianson of the University of Copenhagen analyzed records of over 7,000 Danish twins. His study, conducted in 1978, shows that, while environment still must be regarded as important in forming criminal behavior, identical twins have better than a 65

---
*Lisa Krieger, "Alcoholism Genes May Aid Diagnosis," *San Francisco Examiner* (April 18, 1990): A-2.

†Mednick Sarnoff, "Crime in the Family Tree," *Psychology Today* (March 1985).

percent chance of having similar criminal records. Christianson suggests that an as yet unknown genetic factor influences three times more identical than fraternal twins to become criminals.

Identical twins have the same inheritance; they are genetic clones. If the genetic theory is correct then the presence of a moral trait, such as meticulous honesty, in one twin should show up in the other regardless of whether or not the two were raised together in the same household and general environment. In the last few years, a number of studies has been reported on identical twins who were raised separately from each other in remarkably different family and social environments. Despite the different backgrounds and the fact that they had no contact with each other, they exhibited similar traits. For instance, if one twin showed unselfish concern for other people's welfare (altruism), the other twin behaved likewise. If one showed sorrow and pity for others (compassion), so did the other. This indicates that the attributes of altruism and compassion are inheritable.

Empathy is the ability to put oneself in another person's shoes and temporarily experience the state and feelings that the other person displays. We empathize because, somehow, we care how the other person feels. While empathy is not a moral act, it is a motivation that may lead to consoling or helping a fellow human being, and that is a moral act. Researchers observed babies eighteen months old seeming to care how another baby feels. Toddlers witnessing another's crying show concern and worry. Some psychologists believe that empathy is innate. During the first six years early emergent empathy develops into what is considered moral behavior. Empathy may be the earliest precursor of moral development.*
Not everyone agrees that moral development begins early in life. Some students of child development believe that young children are incapable of moral reasoning and that moral behavior is only readily observable and active in early adolescence.

Hormones, the complex chemical secretions of the endocrine glands, are of critical importance to psychosomatic functioning. Some twenty of these hormones have been identified. Researchers have estimated that 200 or more will ultimately be discovered. Irregularities in hormone supplies—too much or too little—may dramatically alter growth, emotions, attitudes, general health, and moral behavior. Too much of the male sex hormone, testosterone, can contribute to a life of crime or to obsession with sex.

---

*Joseph Alpiers, "Is Empathy Innate?" *This World* (May 19, 1985).

Too much adrenaline, a natural stimulant produced by the adrenal glands, can cause such reactions as combativeness, depression, shyness, and loss of appetite.*

The surrogate mother in the famous Baby M case made a contract to bear a baby for a childless couple. In the beginning all parties to the contract were satisfied with the terms set forth. Months later when Baby M was born, the biological mother refused to give up the baby because of a great wave of unforeseen mother love, which she had not anticipated. The broken contract was devastating to all concerned. Legal battles took place, resulting in much unhappiness. All of the people involved were probably victims of the surrogate mother's high mothering drive, which, possibly was brought on by an oxytocin reaction to a pituitary gland secretion.

Every year brings more research that links organic factors to behaviors we had taken for granted as being derivative of environmental conditioning. This has troubled some people who feel we are starting to lay a foundation of verifiable inherited traits that will eventually downgrade the dominant position of environment as the major cause of mental diseases, (schizophrenia, for example), crime, and other ills of individuals and society. If through accelerating genetic research we are finally forced to accept the tremendous effect of heredity on human behavior, what will it do to the reshaping of behavioral science theory and practice? It is almost certain to intensify the nature-nurture controversy. We may come to see ourselves and our social conventions, morals, laws, and institutions as influenced as much by nature as by nurture.

I am convinced that growing evidence proves that some individuals inherit a "talent" for being civilized, while others inherit a "bad person" complex. The inheritance of moral propensities may evolve more rapidly in one culture than another, in one time frame than another, in one family than another. Moreover, many things can happen genetically to weaken or enhance a trait: for example, interbreeding, or evolution itself.

Most people have a strong distaste for immorality: only the most sadomasochistic or self-destructive among us want to be murdered, robbed, beaten, kidnapped, tortured, held hostage, poisoned, or the like. And there are few, if any, who would admit to liking terrorism or terrorists. The great majority of people, even criminals themselves, have strong aversions to most immoral behaviors. After countless generations of such bitter aversion, can we say for sure that our attitudes toward certain crimes

---

*Timely facts in this paragraph and next are from "Hormones," *Newsweek* (January 12, 1987).

and immoralities have not become an integral part of human nature? It can be illustrated over and over that it is to our advantage to be moral and that morality is necessary for survival. In populations where certain desirable behaviors are continually being reinforced through education and environmental conditioning, these behaviors may become incorporated in genetic mechanisms and passed down from parent to child. Perhaps this is true of what we call conscience. The roots of morality are indeed diverse. As time goes on, the science of genetics may well reveal other potential linkages to moral tendencies.

12

Intellect Versus Emotion, Belief, and Habit in Human Nature

A commonly held idea is that we should be ruled by our intellects rather than by our emotions. The forces of intelligence and feelings are often depicted as being at war with each other. One generally accepted explanation is that the evolution of our emotions was fairly well completed and stabilized when brain development was beginning a rapid evolutionary jump upward. An important component of this view is that, whereas our emotions are crude, intense, animalistic, and exceedingly primitive, our more recent acquisition of sophisticated intelligence is not only being regularly overruled by emotional motivations, but has become the willing servant of the animal in us. This theory comes in handy in explaining our inhumanity toward one another, which can be documented by thousands of unbelievably horrifying examples drawn from virtually any period in history: the present-day massacres and terrorism of the Middle East; the gasoline-soaked flaming tire necklaces of South African radicals; the predatory behavior of Genghis Khan, the Mongol conqueror; Hitler's holocaust; and any war one can name.

These large-scale, monstrous inhumanities required the diligent use of our prized attributes: among them, intelligence, cooperative skills, planning abilities, inventiveness, persistence of purpose, and many others. As we look back on the endless catalogue of inhuman enterprises, they seem utterly outrageous. They meet every definition of insanity and psychosis. Yet, the planners of these actions rationalize their barbarism as necessary to the achievement of what others regard as spurious and irrational goals.

Established moral principles are treated as relative and elastic, to be used or abused to gain private ends. In fact, to them their very goals may be blessed, as in the case of *jihad* or holy war. Killing infidels and heretics has been practiced by every modern religion at sometime in its history. It is unbelievable that the atrocities of history were all solely the result of emotions gone wild. They were as likely to be quests for power or social and economic revolution with little or no consideration given to the many people who paid for them with suffering and death. Political, economic, and social revolutions usually employ armed conflict, most of which is rationalized, even by religion, as a moral struggle against immorality.

Not much evidence supports the notion that humans have made further evolutionary advances in the last few thousand years. Knowledge was extremely slow in developing. In the last century humans have learned more than in all preceding time put together. We have acquired great skill in using our intelligence but not much skill in using and controlling our emotions. Evolution is very slow. Someday it may even be possible to speed up our emotional evolution.

No general agreement exists on what we humans are by nature. We can describe our behavior but not our nature. If we strip away our cultural attributes, the results of learning and experience, what are we? Are we fundamentally good, kind, sympathetic, tender, compassionate, and loving? If so, why do we demonstrate so much vindictiveness, hate, hostility, rage, greed, jealousy, envy, and aggression? Surely, we are a mix of all these emotional propensities.

Perhaps we are incapable of being anything apart from our environment. It is the environment to which we react and these reactions involve our neuroendocrinal biochemistry and all our other physiological processes. Perhaps we have no nature or disposition or anything separate and apart from our milieu or environment. We are a "something" so long as we are conscious, but in death we are nothing. When we are conscious of ourselves, we are simultaneously aware of other aspects of our environment: our internal environment of mind and feeling, and our external environment, which we must learn to use and master and force with thought and effort to yield the means of survival. It is in that reciprocity of internal and external environment that we discover ourselves and the meaning of morality.

Humans never had a nature apart from their interaction with the external environment. All our human drives, desires, and appetites that are biological in origin are shared by other animals. Now consider our competitiveness, our aggressiveness, and our anger over being imprisoned, compelled, or forced; all of these characteristics are also possessed in some degree by other sentient life forms. Charles Darwin considered morality the one uniquely human trait. This is hard to accept unquestionably since humankind spends as much ingenuity in violating or avoiding morality as in following its principles. But, then consider the matter of love, caring, responsibility, and respect; tender feelings such as sympathy, compassion, and empathy; and socially constructive inclinations to cooperate, give, help, and so on. These are by no means distinctly human but they are more developed and prominently displayed by we humans and, no doubt, gained us the self-congratulatory reputation of being a higher animal.

Behavioral scientists agree that humankind is far and away the most intelligent life form. This, then, is the only genuinely unique ingredient of what we call human nature. It is our intelligence more than any other attribute that can be credited with having created our science and technology; moral philosophy, law, government, administrative skills, religion, and educational institutions; graphic and plastic arts, performing arts, the art and science of medicine; and, of course, the ability to survive despite our self-destructiveness and the capacity to build civilization faster than we can destroy it. Also, our intelligence brought us the nuclear dilemma. Now new dilemmas are shaping: overpopulation and overutilization of natural resources. We are about to learn again that intellect cannot be the servant of desire, but its master.

Now I shall direct attention to the matter of habit and belief in moral life. Habit is the result of doing something so often that it becomes automatic. Psychologists have defined memory as merely doing the thing learned. Once we have learned and practiced tying our shoes, for example, we can tie them without conscious thought. At this stage we call the automatic tying a habit. Habit then turns out to be just an example of memory, which is merely doing the learned thing. Closely related to habit is belief, which bears allegiance to decision. If I decide, say, that God exists, or if during my upbringing I am taught that God exists, then it can be said that I believe in God.

The process of acculturation is largely a matter of acquiring habits and beliefs. These regulators of daily living are learned early and late, but mostly early. Preferences in food; personal grooming; taste in theater, literature, and music; in fact, many basic preferences and aversions are established early in the course of growing up. They occur first in the family circle, then in school and at play, in religious training, and so on. Moral education runs through all of these experiences. As we become older and experience higher levels of formal education, social exposure, travel, and aesthetic stimulation, old habits and preferences could be modified to a great extent, even dropped from our repertoire of beliefs and habitual behaviors. However, some old beliefs and habits may cling to us, unmodified, to the end.

Some psychologists are convinced that experiencing strong beliefs (or believing) is one of the things we humans do best. The brain mechanisms for changing beliefs exist, according to Michael S. Gazzaniga,* but established beliefs are hard to change. This could be a powerful factor in the slow changing of society. Once moral concepts and systems are set up in an individual or society, they do not yield readily to renovation, substitution, and change. Gazzaniga argues that beliefs exist because we have a need for consistency and reliability. Americans can easily observe the interlinking of reliability and belief, for even though we are a pluralistic society, splintered into a multitude of political, economic, religious, and social sects, our saving grace is a common belief in the reliability of democracy, our constitution, and the legal system. This is the cement that holds us together for the time being, not the Bible or the Koran or the Talmud.

It takes a lot of discord and confusion—what Gazzaniga calls "dissonance"†—in a society to bring about the serious questioning of beliefs. No one expects an Islamic leader to give up his beliefs and embrace Judaism, nor the pope to go over to the side of secular humanism. It would take an overwhelming amount of dissonance to bring that about. But have no fear that dissonance is fading; it is at present widespread and growing. Many beliefs about our institutions and our morality are losing ground. Here is just a small sampling of the recent confusion: the aftermath of the 1987 stock market crash, the irresponsible government policies that have made us the world's greatest debtor nation, the political justification of stopgap social programs on the basis of highly questionable moral assumptions, politicians intimating that moral rectitude motivates their obvious power plays and appeals to voters for support, and the exposure of deceptive practices in the television empire of certain Christian fundamentalist organizations. Dozens of these dangerous signals indicate that the moral fabric of society is unraveling, that once common beliefs are retreating from usage.

The Social Brain (New York: Basic Books, 1985), pp. 3ff.

†Psychological dissonance, first described by Gazzaniga's colleague Leon Festinger, refers to a state of conflict "between a held belief and actual behavior" wherein "something has to give," *The Social Brain*, p. 80.

Beliefs may be the outgrowth of our search for safety and reliability. If so, then we understand the joy of the religious convert who builds an ideological fortress on faith. However, if promises of fulfillment are not realized, a system of beliefs may turn to doubt and skepticism, which are the flipside of belief and relative certainty. These contending forces seem to be at work in us most of the time as we weigh pros and cons in the decisions we make. Moral decision making would be tremendously simplified if we could create a universally acceptable, science-based moral code. I introduce a theory for doing this in Part Three.

When our beliefs are questioned or criticized, we will usually react defensively and our defenses are often accompanied by feelings of resentment, anger, and anxiety. We may describe ourselves as having been insulted. It is possible for a psychological insult to be as painful to the recipient as a physical wound, an insult to the flesh. This is another powerful reason that moral discourse is generally unpopular. It is difficult to get a consensus of opinion, let alone agreement, in the discussion of moral issues. This is another way in which emotions turn the tide against intellect and reason.

It takes a great deal of time for reason to win out over beliefs and the emotional reaction to their challenge. In 1988, the United States government apologized to Americans of Japanese descent who were interned during World War II. It took our government half a century to admit officially that our beliefs concerning the potential for treasonous behavior among Japanese-Americans were ill-founded. Those loyal Americans lived with traumatic insult far too long.

Everyday citizens are a reservoir of unconfirmed and unproven beliefs. Here are a few examples:

Money is the root of all evil.

Our elected legislators represent us.

The Earth is far from being overpopulated.

Government should provide the greatest good for the greatest number.

Enterprise for profit is morally inferior to nonprofit enterprise.

Rights are God-given.

Majority rule is wiser than minority rule.

All of these statements are opinions, not confirmed facts.

As a people we are not presently equipped to solve the burdensome moral problems that confront us. In fact, we find difficulty in defining the problems. We do not know anymore about poverty, for example, than the ancient Greeks. We will most likely attempt to solve the problem of poverty by methods used unsuccessfully many times in history. We can modernize the methods of Robin Hood, the twelfth-century outlaw who, with his merry men of legendary Sherwood Forest, robbed the rich to feed the poor. We are capable of doing this even though what is purported to have worked in a feudal ecosystem will not work in the human ecology of the twentieth century. Many politicians are willing to support unproven policies and to practice deceit, fraud, and robbery under such rubrics as value-added taxes, excise taxes, corporation taxes, progressive taxes, and so on. We are buried under worn-out beliefs and moral misconceptions. Perhaps what we really do best is hang on to the belief that all social ills can be cured through spending and taxation.

In Part Two I have attempted to show what moral principles are, how they originated, and how they were shaped by human experiences and institutions. Additionally, I have pointed out how the morality of society is influenced by certain of our biological characteristics, such as our susceptibility to drugs; our responses to nutrition; our variations in mental and physical health; our individual behavioral characteristics stemming from heredity and environment; and the conflicts of emotion, intellect, and belief.

I have no more than touched on some of the important factors in the shaping and development of moral principles. With so much information at hand, it would have been easy for me to linger on moral history, hereditary influences, or other subjects pertinent to the shaping of morals, but then I would have been distracted from my main concern which is the presentation of a fresh approach to morals.

I have emphasized that morals are the backbone of culture and civilization. No matter how tough and retrogressive the human experience, morality and civilization hangs on. That is why we are still here, and if some day we are no longer here, it will be because we lost moral control of our destiny. No one can lay claim to being civilized who is not moral. A civilized nation or community is one in which individuals are true to themselves and to each other, assume moral responsibility for themselves, and, collectively, assume moral responsibility for each other.

Part Three

Moral Principles and Models for Our Times

13

Is a Simple, Comprehensive System of Morals Possible?

I believe it is possible to formulate a system of moral analysis that is both simple and comprehensive. Such a system should be universally applicable and capable of solving moral problems of any nature. Also, I am convinced that a science of morals is possible. I know of no one who has discovered and reported in print a genuine science of morals. Ethics is defined as a science of morals.* It is doubtful, however, that many present-day ethicists and moral philosophers agree with this.

How does moral knowledge stand today as a science? Not very well, I'm afraid. Since the time of Socrates and Plato, moral philosophers have created a prodigious body of organized ideas, theories, and systems. They have carefully examined and defined moral principles with amazing ingenuity and logical virtuosity. Their products have profoundly influenced the state, politics, law, and the public acceptance of certain social and political ideas, such as a just society, majority rule, liberty, political revolutions, human rights, duty and social responsibility, the common good of all, socialism, capitalism, the redistribution of wealth, the abolition of poverty, and on and on. Moral philosophy has made a great contribution to human well-being, but it has failed to bring forth proven theories and a verifiable body of scientific knowledge that is universally accepted and used, as is true, to a great extent, in the physical sciences.

---

*Oxford Dictionary of the English Language, 1933, 2nd ed. (Oxford: Clarendon Press, 1989). Ethics is also defined as a scheme of moral science.

It seems to be an unwritten law of history that no sooner is a scientific theory advanced than exceptions crop up. Exceptions to the workability of a theory prove fatal to that theory if the exception is substantiated and provable. This rule will undoubtedly be applied to the moral theories advanced herein.

As early as the thirteenth century, Thomas Aquinas (1225-1274) advanced the idea that moral law is natural law based on human nature and that it is discoverable by reason. He believed humankind possesses natural goodness and that justice, prudence, temperance, and fortitude were natural virtues. Obviously, Aquinas did not derive moral law from what we would term verifiable, scientific methods. Even John Locke (1632-1704), the father of the experimental methods of modern science, believed that morals could be determined apart from scientific methods. To this day, by and large, moral thought has eluded scientific discipline and study.

During the last hundred years the science of psychology has made a few important contributions to moral knowledge, particularly to the fields of moral development and education. Impressive, long-term studies on the moral development of people from early childhood through late adulthood have been made in the twentieth century by psychologists Jean Piaget, Erik H. Erikson, Robert J. Havighurst, Jane Loeoinger, Carol Gilligan, and especially by Laurence Kohlberg, whose monumental research on moral development was conducted in widely scattered populations throughout the world. Researchers who pioneered the psychology of moral development have made surprisingly corroborating and brilliant discoveries concerning the moral perspectives and behaviors of individuals at various stages of life. Convincing evidence has been presented showing that moral thinking and behaviors change and grow through specific stages of development—from childhood through adolescence, adulthood, and old age—in a somewhat uniform manner from culture to culture throughout the world. These findings suggest that certain moral principles are universal despite the absence of anything resembling a universal moral code. A general agreement seems to declare that, if individuals fail to learn a given moral principle or behavior at the usual stage of development for that particular task, they may have difficulty learning and adjusting to subsequent moral learning tasks at later, more advanced stages of development. This suggests that the neglect of moral education during early stages of moral development will hinder countless thousands from acquiring socially useful moral knowledge and behavior.*

---

*For details see J. M. Rich and J. L. De Vitis, *Theories of Moral Development* (Springfield, Ill.: Charles C. Thomas, 1985).

Is a Simple, Comprehensive System of Morals Possible? 77

Psychologists have tended to accept commonly held moral ideas and concepts in their research. As far as I can determine, no psychological theories of morality have been developed or researched. Individual behaviors like stealing and deceit have been seriously investigated by psychologists. In general, the study of the nature of morality has been neglected by scientists, leaving this challenging field largely to moral philosophers.

Psychologists' innovations in the field of moral development have opened the way for more effective curriculum planning for the teaching of morals, from the first grade of elementary school through college. A major concern of educational psychologists has been how people learn at different stages of development and when they are most ready to learn certain subjects and skills. It seems to me that educational psychology, as a field of endeavor, has concentrated less on determining what moral concepts and behaviors should be taught than on determining when and how such subject matter should be taught. But could the situation be otherwise in a culture encumbered by the morality maze and the absence of a widely accepted science-based system of morality?

Specialists in linguistics, the scientific study of language, have investigated the forms and functions of language in communication about ethics, morals, the criteria for making judgments, and the making of choices, all of which are deemed important in decision making. Interest in the role of language in moral theory has been growing since the philosopher C. L. Stevenson published *Ethics and Language* in 1934.*

In striking out for new moral territory, I have set aside the burden of accounting for the intricate, varied, esoteric, and vast moral discourse of the past. Others have recently tamed this literature and brought it into the range of understanding by ordinary people. An excellent example is Richard Taylor's *Good and Evil* (1985).† This frees me to go on with my explorations without any affront to my worthy predecessors.

My search for a rational foundation for the scientific study of morals led me to the life sciences, more particularly to biology, and still more particularly to human ecology. The science of ecology, a branch of biology, grew from the scientific truth that no form of life can exist, be studied,

---

*For two modern, but quite different linguistic approaches to moral thought, compare Mary Forrester's *Moral Language* (Madison: University of Wisconsin Press, 1982) with Timothy J. Cooney's *Telling Right from Wrong* (Buffalo, N.Y.: Prometheus Books, 1985). I found these books absorbing but of little guidance in laying out a simple science-based theory of morals.

†Buffalo, N.Y.: Prometheus Books.

or be understood apart from its environment. Applied to humans, as well as to other organisms, ecology is the study of the interaction of organisms with the totality of their environment(s).

The term *ecology* was first used by the German scientist Ernest Haeckel in 1869. It stems from the Greek word *oikos* "house" and *logos* "knowledge"; means a knowledge of our home. Since the early 1960s, ecology has grown into a large field of inquiry with many branches and specialties, one of which is human ecology.

In Part Two, I introduced an ecological theory of morals. Leading features of this theory were revealed. I demonstrated that moral principles are discoveries, not inventions; that they are reactions to human biological requisites such as survival, life maintenance, and social organization (government); that they are as essential to life as physiological systems; and that moral knowledge consists of objective, not relative principles. This statement is a partial answer to the question that begins this chapter.

The natural setting for a science of morality is human ecology. The discovery and utilization of moral behavior was and still is an inevitable biological event without which we would not exist. This process makes the continuity of human life possible. It continues in our relentless search for answers to grave new bioenvironmental problems, which are the basic subject matter of this book. Moral behavior is the natural regulator of human relations, pervading all our interactions. It is impossible to describe a moral act without considering environmental factors. It is also impossible to understand an organism's environment without perceiving it as functionally integrated with the organism. In the next chapter I shall examine the main components of human environment as a frame of reference for the exposition of an ecological theory of morals.

14

The Human Environment

The human environment has three basic components: (1) the inner world of mind, beliefs, personal needs, sensations, drives, emotions, traits, and attitudes; (2) other humans; and (3) the outer world of natural phenomena, whether organic (biotic) or inorganic (abiotic). The third component supplies us with the basic needs of existence: air, water, nutrition, and habitat. So dependent are we on the physical environment that space travel requires us to take the essentials of our environment with us. Without the presence of others, we could not even dream of having a rewarding life. Yet, this very presence creates interpersonal problems, the moral solution of which determines the difference between barbarism and civilization. The quality of our inner world of body and mind is closely linked to the quality of our adaptation to the outer world of people, things, and events.

We rarely think of ourselves as a part of our environment. This organism that is us is endowed with a brain, sensory organs, memory, feelings, drives, and much more. We have intelligence, thoughts, problem-solving ability, beliefs, dreams, desires, preferences and many other characteristics. In addition, we have powerful drives, such as hunger, sex, and self-preservation, coupled with our common desire for freedom, adventure, risk taking, acquisitiveness, affection, play, security, and self-expression. All of this adds up to our inner environment, a personal realm that is not readily accessible to others, and that even we ourselves find difficult to know in all its complexity. Unfortunately, we must add to our inner environment all of our negative characteristics, such as destructiveness, fierceness, hostility, cruelty, greed, and a lust for power and control over others and what they produce. This inner environment also includes all our physiological and biochemical processes as well as the suffering and pain that goes with being human. All that we are as a work of nature must be considered an important component of environment whenever that term is used.

Continuing with the inner world theme, I shall call attention to feelings and emotions that sometimes are erroneously equated with moral thought. For example, distressful feelings and emotions, such as envy, jealousy, grief, sorrow, guilt, shame, anxiety, fear, rage, and hate have no direct bearing on morality, but are frequently regarded as having moral implications. For instance, though grief is regarded as a normal or moral response to losing a loved one, acting out the feeling of rage may, if harmful, be abnormal or immoral. Acting out a feeling of envy has frequently led to murder. It is what we do in response to our feelings that can be moral or immoral, not the feelings themselves. Likewise, benign feelings, such as affection, love, joy, laughter, sex, gratitude, and gladness do not in and of themselves generate moral or immoral acts. Harmful practical jokes are not born of a sense of humor alone, and sex crimes are not caused by sexual feelings alone.

Certain feelings and emotions become associated with both moral and immoral acts. I am concerned that we do not confuse them with moral thought or make moral judgments based solely on personal feelings and emotions. Humans are both thinking and feeling creatures. Feelings and emotions are important primitive, adaptive mechanisms. Some of them prepare us to fight or flee for the sake of protection or survival, while others prepare us for friendly and affectionate encounters. It is generally accepted that these powerful motivators evolved earlier than high intelligence and thinking ability. This may be why we are told so often to curb our impulses and think before acting. Moral training and knowledge are not only antidotes for impulsiveness, but they open the way to more socially effective moral decision making than would hasty interpretations of highly charged emotional information.

Media news, entertainment, and advertising are loaded with emotionally charged political and public policy propaganda. Earlier, I wrote at some length on the subject of how we are being manipulated emotionally by word magic. In 1984 we were awash in the "fairness-unfairness" issue. These buzzwords were joined by the holy of holies, "compassion." By 1988 the most fashionable buzzwords were "sensitive" and "insensitive." Through usage, meanings were given to them that were not intended in their original definitions and usage. Several examples follow.

The word *insensitive* means without senses, unfeeling, perhaps anesthetized. No such thing exists as a sensitive issue, cause, or subject because these things do not have sense organs. Why do literate speakers and writers speak of the inanimate as sensitive or insensitive? It is a veiled way of declaring that the issue, cause, or subject is controversial. When we declare a person to be insensitive, we simply mean that the individual is opposed to our moral or political position. Writers and speakers on political and social matters who use "sensitive" and "insensitive" weaken the point they are trying to make by substituting a vague generalization for down-to-earth facts. Why say of a certain senator that he is insensitive, when what is meant is that he is opposed to deficit spending on social programs. If the agent means that the senator is hardhearted, then let the speaker say so. In politics it seems more sensible to be sensitive than insensitive. In moral discourse the word means nothing; it can and should be avoided.

Compassion is another word that masquerades as a moral imperative. A politician who invites being regarded as lacking compassion is committing political suicide. Compassion has two sides: pleading a case (seeking compassion) and coercing consent (for lack of compassion). Like compassion, *pity* should not be a factor in making a moral decision. There is no end to our capacity for a show of hand-wringing compassion and pity. This makes for good political theater, but inept decisions. *Empathy*, identifying oneself with another, is in a class with compassion and pity. Attributing to another our own feelings is sometimes referred to as the *pathetic fallacy*. (*Pathetic* for sadness and *fallacy* for not really knowing how the other guy feels.) *Sympathy*, an affinity for the feelings or predicament of another, means we understand how others feel and are sorry. *Sorry* means that we recognize what has gone awry but can do nothing about it. In the classical sense sorry means full of impotent sorrow and pity. *Altruism*, the desire to want to help others, is, perhaps, a noble attribute, but like the others mentioned above, its efficacy is utterly dependent on knowing what to do that will be helpful, and having the skill and means to do it.

We have been pursuing a description of our inner environment. What goes on in there is not known or felt by others unless we communicate it through specific behaviors. Thus, it would be impossible to commit a moral or immoral act by thoughts and feelings that take place in the privacy of our minds. However, the reverse holds when we express through behavior (verbal or nonverbal) our inner world of thought and feeling. We immediately bring our behavior to the attention of others and open it to the interpretation and responses of others, for better or worse. This brings us to consider thoroughly the outer environment of others, the second component of human environment.

An interaction occurs between the inner environment of self and the outer environment of others. They influence each other. Benefits as well as harm move between the two. In fact, moral principles themselves arise from the interaction of the inner and outer worlds. The powerful motivators of the inner world are triggered by the events of the outer world. Once stimulated into being, the motivators spur people on to make behavioral decisions. We need to remind ourselves that emotions and other motivators are never in and of themselves immoral. It is the individual's reactions to emotions, desires, drives, traits, and attitudes that are the concern of morality, not the motivators themselves.

We are seldom unaware of our inner world of self and the outer world of others. We are aware that others by the billions are out there and that their activities, interests, creative powers, friendliness, and, sometimes, malevolence influence us even from the far corners of the earth. The effects of those others who are close by are stronger than those who are far away, though we may be activated by the latter when they threaten acts of war and terrorism. We are acutely aware of those close by; they are our relatives, friends, and helpers. A few of those close by can be dangerous. Otherwise, people as a whole seem benign.

The outer environment of others is what we call society: the nations, cities, and organizations of every kind; laborers, manufacturers, builders, farmers, creators; the worlds of art, education, religion, government, economics; in fact, everything with which an encyclopedia is packed. A vast territory within the environment of others is especially important to an understanding of morals, and that is the area of ideas, concepts, and beliefs, such as prejudices, superstitions, conventions, ethical and moral codes, as well as political and legal systems. Taken collectively, they constitute the essence of civilization.

No more than one hundred years ago, the world consisted of several specific ethnic and cultural regions, each with its own unique character. Today, due to the communications and transportation technology revolution, all this worldwide cultural diversity is drawn more closely together, where, for the first time in history, peoples are quickly learning about each other and, in some instances, feeling forced to preserve traditional customs, religions, and lifestyles at great economic and social cost. The contemporary morality maze results in good measure from a daily crisscrossing of transcultural highways with the concomitant clashing of many ideas from continent to continent.

We are in a new situation where conflicting standards of morals and behavior produce tensions between groups within states and between nations. This can lead to disastrous misunderstandings and dangerous international problems, as well as fruitless political bickering at local levels. We are truly at a crossroads of morality. What a boon a science of morals would be, and what a boost it would be to the development of a universally accepted moral code! However, the impediments to this seem endless: rigid customs and laws, deeply embedded beliefs, and the thought-control power of all organizations concerned with social policy and with propagating themselves. All seem to stand in the way.

People are engaged in decision making in nearly everything they do, and morals are frequently used in such decision scenarios. Decision making requires varying degrees of effort. We usually do not expend effort unless a possible reward is forthcoming. The goal of practically every decision is a profit or advantage of some kind. We tend to question the sanity of a person who deliberately decides to lose or forgo something. While the intent of a decision may be as simple as gaining a profit, the act of making the decision may be complicated by the consideration of many facts, such as risks, advantages, effects on the various people involved, one's reputation, and so on. It is hard to imagine a decision that excludes human relations. This, of course, ushers in moral considerations. No matter what we decide, if it affects us, it will certainly affect others, and this brings us to the heart of morality.

Of tremendous importance to the development of an ecological theory of morals is the concept of identification. Like believing, identification is one of the things we humans do best. And we do it frequently, from the beginning to the end of our lives. We identify with all those things in our environment of self, others, and the material world that have a bearing on our welfare as living organisms.

We learn to regard people and material objects as being related to us in some way, or ourselves as being related to them. At a certain stage of development, we differentiate our parents from other men and women. As we come to discriminate one person from another, we see ourselves as separate, as individuals. At this stage of growth and development, we begin to use such personal pronouns as "I," "me," "my," and "mine." We learn our relationship to others and to the things around us. We say "my mother," "my house," "my school," and "this bike or this home is mine."

Identification is the giant social security blanket of childhood. It is a part of growing up and the formation of personality. Starting with family, friends, school, and religious training, identifications continue outward from this center into the community, the state, the nation, a vocation, a college, social organizations, political parties, and, perhaps, one world. In establishing our own identity we find security in the growth of our ability to assume responsibility for ourselves, a primary moral learning task. After a period of identifying with colleges or job experiences, we may marry and have a family, or find a still different center of life that provides our major relationships.

The identification process is evidence that we come to perceive some aspects of our environment as extensions of ourselves, as a necessary and advantageous part of ourselves—in a biological sense. This leads us to the conviction that these objects in our total environment with which we identify even belong to us, that they are ours or are related to us in some way.

In this way, it seems sensible to speak of *my* child, *my* family, or *my* employer even though we do not lay any claim to owning them. Also, it is established usage to speak of belonging to a certain group even though membership in the group does not imply that we are owned by it, as a piece of property might be owned. However, when it comes to things like cars or bank accounts, with which we also identify, saying *my* car or *my* bank account *does* imply ownership. Whenever we use the pronouns *my* or *mine* we serve notice that we are identified with the object following the pronoun, that we are related to it in some way, or that we have some claim on (or right to) the object. The more we talk about identification, the more our attention is directed to interpersonal relations and personal property, both of which are outcomes of identification.

Just as beliefs are hard to shake, so are identifications. Once formed they tend to stick. Relationships last. Hanging on to our property may at times become our most important objective. Trouble begins when others encroach on our property, weaken the safety of our interpersonal affiliations, or alienate our sources of affection and goodwill. Identifications can be both strong and long-lasting: many people would rather die than risk losing their beliefs or their properties. But beliefs and identifications have some striking differences as well. For instance, property in all forms can be stolen or destroyed, whereas beliefs are not subject to such a fate.

In its broadest sense, property is based on the realities of biological existence. We are our own property: we own and belong to ourselves. We identify with what we create and behave toward our creations as our property. Humans often fight to the death for their survival and the survival of loved ones; sometimes they will even risk their lives to protect material property. As we push ahead, property of all kinds will be seen as a necessary and inevitable constituent of human ecology and as a core factor in moral law.

I have briefly reviewed the essential facts and concepts of the first two basic components of the human environment: our inner world of body and mind and the outer world of others. Now it's time to discuss the third basic component.

Everything humankind is and does depends on the natural environment of the planet. This statement introduces my brief account of the third component of our environment, the natural (biotic and abiotic) phenomena that envelop and nurture us.

The term *mother earth* suggests an inviting, caring habitat. Actually, the earth is not especially inviting or caring, or even nurturing were it not for the existence of other life forms, plants and animals, upon which we have been as dependent as we have been upon the earth itself. Of course, our physical surroundings provide for and support us, as well as other organisms, but early on it wasn't easy. Life was tough for primitive humans. As much as ninety percent of our ancestors' waking hours were spent on food gathering and protecting themselves from the elements. Nature could be pretty nasty with heat and cold, rain and snow, drought, storms, and wildfires to say nothing of the trials brought on by the ice ages.

While other creatures adapted to the natural environment, humans learned to alter and modify their immediate environment to make living safer and more comfortable. And we are still in the process of subduing nature. Today, we have reached (some say "evolved" to) a point at which the physical world has been altered to such a great extent that restoration of the earth to its prehuman condition would be practically impossible. Our continuous search for a better life is using up natural resources at a prodigious and alarming rate. Worse yet, we have set in motion such dangerous processes that we may not be able to stop their destructive potential.

We needn't look far to find ample illustration of some actual and potential man-made disasters. Our rivers and lesser streams have been polluted to such an extent that no potable water is available from them anywhere on earth except in the most remote regions. In the continental United States few streams afford safe drinking water. Ecological systems important to our well-being have been destroyed; climate has been altered; the protective Antarctic ozone layer in the upper atmosphere has been breached; the air we breathe has been polluted; the increase in carbon dioxide (a by-product of combustion) in the earth's atmosphere could create a "greenhouse" weather change that will melt the polar ice caps which, in turn, will raise the sea level, flooding coastal cities throughout the globe; and the control of plants and insects with herbicides and insecticides is backfiring. Overpopulation, disease, famine, and war are part of the picture, and this is not all.

If this were not enough, we are overcutting forests: great green belts like the Amazon rain forests are being rapidly harvested for hardwood and cleared for farming. The reduction of living plants coupled with increases in fossil fuel use are steadily reducing oxygen levels in the atmosphere. The burning of coal to produce electric power is adding to the air pollution that causes acid rain, which has been linked to damage caused to large areas of vegetation in North America and Europe. Dependable evidence indicates that we are overdrawing on all our natural resources, particularly on food supplies from the world's oceans. There is no doubt that we are despoiling nature, but no more flagrantly than our self-degradation through crime, drug addiction, neglect of personal health, war, terrorism, nuclear radiation poisoning, and other sociopolitical examples of collective lack of will.

These threats to the inhabitants of the planet will sooner or later be well known by the general population and we shall be forced to make decisions for change; otherwise we will perish or live on in miserable want. When we finally discover a way out of the mess, we will have discovered that self-interest is an element of moral ecology. An interest in survival is genuine self-interest. It manifests itself in many ways, one of which is to preserve and protect our environment. We are not without knowledge of what to do, just how to do it. A higher and higher price will have to be paid if we allow our environment to continue its present rate of deterioration into the middle of the next century. That price will not only include economic sacrifice, but the forfeiture of an entire style of life together with its accompanying emotional adjustment and changes in self-management of desires, wants, and needs.

We are not accustomed to thinking of ourselves as being integrally locked by biological forces to our outer environment of others and our habitat. A move cannot be made in one of the three components of environment without its being felt in the other two. The time is coming when our inner environment must change from customary wants and gratifications to enlightened self-interest and responsible concern for the lives around us and the natural world. Great changes in the inner world of human expectations and attitudes must precede the effective control of population growth, poverty, unemployment and, of course, the rescue of our earth from further degradation. The latter must head the list of our priorities.

In the United States, a combination of private-sector organizations, legislative activity, educational efforts, and growing popular demand have brought forth a strong environmental protection and rehabilitation movement. An expanding body of environmental law and many regulatory agencies have been established. Some aspects of the movement advanced rapidly, particularly the development of rules and regulations. These have not always been enthusiastically received by big business, real estate developers, manufacturers, and even some government agencies. Everyone has probably heard of the hated environmental impact report and the attempts to save endangered life forms, such as the now famous snail darter.

Despite welcome progress, we are not moving toward solutions as fast as new problems arise. When people at the grassroots level participate in conservation, cease polluting the environment, take adequate care of themselves, drive responsibly on streets and highways, willingly assume personal responsibility for harm done to others and to society, and show respect for each others' privacy and privileges, we will know that significant progress is underway. Finally, waste recycling; the eventual disappearance of smoking in public places; and the end of littering our public streets, freeways, and parks will signal that society is ready to take seriously the need to create a safe and sound environment.

Nature appears to be amoral. The food chain, a central subject of ecology, is full of horror stories. Sea urchins eat plankton, sea worms eat urchins, fish eat worms, birds eat fish, and so on. Even some plants subsist on insects and small animals. Ultimately, as the millennia pass, life forms achieve a balance. For example, rapidly proliferating field mice will destroy their food supply, a field of grasses, and many die until all that's left is a dwindling band of starving mice. Plant life in the rodents' domain gradually makes a comeback and the cycle of population growth and decline starts over again. This dog-eat-dog, this-eat-that world demonstrates that nature not only knows best but operates according to unified bioenvironmental principles. Each life form, including humans, exists because it gives top priority to self-preservation, which, of course, is the subject matter of ecological horror stories. All creatures do what is necessary and advantageous for their survival. This is the natural way of all living things and human beings are no exception.

The twentieth century has witnessed the greatest draw on natural, nonrenewable resources of any period in history. Thoughtless damage to the environment was beginning to show up in the first quarter of the century. Sewage and waste disposal as well as air pollution and water contamination became serious problems in our large cities and manufacturing centers. An accompanying clamor commenced for public health regulation of meat packing, food processing, drug manufacturing, and sanitation. The last quarter of this century has brought us to a crisis point in public health, environmental contamination, overexploitation of natural resources, and a sudden surge in population growth. The great danger of resource overuse will continue unabated until overpopulation is not merely controlled but reversed. Reversal should continue until demand and resource supplies are brought back into balance. If such a course is not taken, worldwide excessive use of resources will become more disadvantageous for humankind with each passing year. When the environment strikes back and threatens us with the deprivation of necessities and advantages, we will quickly arrive at the profound moral conviction that overpopulation and concomitant resource overdraft are immoral.

When the capacity of the environment to support humans has been exceeded in one or more ways over a number of years, people will begin to feel the threat. Some areas will experience severe shortages of certain foods and pure water; others will be exposed to toxic poisoning; or the sickening stress of overpopulation, unemployment, increasing poverty, and other distressing conditions. Such an environmental predicament, when it comes, will be accompanied by a decline in biological necessities and advantages. When this point has been reached, what will guide the decisions of government and society? Will chaos be the order of the day? A worldwide calamity has never been faced. No moral formula exists for handling one. The sharing and rationing of necessities would fail: even at current annual world food production levels, if all the food supplies for a given year were equally divided among all the world's people, some would starve and the rest would suffer malnutrition. The moral implications of such dilemmas will be dealt with later in Part Three.

15

The Moral Lessons of Catastrophes

Humankind is preparing a series of future calamities, among them overpopulation, irreparable damage to habitat, and probable nuclear holocaust (glasnost and a united Europe notwithstanding). The media has acquainted us with these potential catastrophes. First, I shall briefly review the highlights of these horrors, then I shall use each as background for illustrating and developing certain moral theories and their functions and limitations.

The first thing to observe is that none of these catastrophes has as yet occurred. Quite obviously, nothing I have to say about their likely outcomes can be based on actual precedent. However, a great deal of study has been given to possible outcomes. Many predictions can be made on the basis of known facts. We might call these informed speculations. Nonetheless, they can help us in our thinking about what can happen and what we can do to avoid the predicted events. Moreover, my aim here is to find out what we can learn about moral theory from this discussion of possible catastrophic events.

At the present rate of world population growth, overpopulation will arrive at a crisis stage before the end of the twenty-first century. When the crisis stage arrives, it will be too late to defuse the population bomb. The fecundity of the planet will have suffered irreparable losses. Escape from mass starvation will not be possible.

Overpopulation is a problem of human ecology. It is in the same family of ecological phenomena as population explosions among field mice. Unchecked population growth is a threat to the survival of any form of life. Field mice die by the thousands when their few acres of habitat are denuded of food. In a similar situation, what will humans do? Are we capable of rescuing ourselves from a population overexpansion before catastrophe arrives? We can be certain of one thing: universal opposition to population growth will have become an ecologically based moral principle. No one will dare to recommend business as usual for human reproductive propensities.

The threat overpopulation poses to our quality of life, if not life itself, will make of population control a moral imperative linked to urgent biological necessities. Population control will become a moral mandate of society. Long before conditions get as bad as my forecast, abortion and all forms of contraception will have ceased being moral and religious issues. They will have become accepted as part of a new sexual moral code.

Japan has led the world in facing and solving an overpopulation problem. The Japanese still have a long way to go before they are self-sufficient in food production. China is among the few highly populated countries that has undertaken an ambitious population reduction program, requiring that no couple have more than one child. Penalties are stiff for failure. Actually, only a few Asian and African countries are capable of producing enough food to feed themselves. Thousands of people around the world starve to death or die of malnutrition every day. Starvation is a direct result of a population outgrowing its traditional sources of food. In 1984–1985 we learned, beyond a doubt, that North Africa had reached such a point. The great desert areas of that region have had a small, widely distributed population for centuries. Such a habitat can only meet modest human requirements. Civil wars and drought upset this delicate balance thus creating the North African catastrophe. Famine is not invariably a measure of overpopulation. For example, drought and an overdependence on potatoes—a strange combination—caused the nineteenth-century Irish famine.

No matter how encouraging the population-control efforts may be regarding China and Japan, the news from the rest of the world is not so positive. At the present time, population growth in underdeveloped and developing countries remains unchecked. The Earth's population is rising at a rate of about two percent per year; or to put it another way, the global population is doubling every thirty-five years. (Figures based on Isaac Asimov's *A Choice of Catastrophes,* 1979.)* By the year 2000,

---

*Population statistics and predictions given here are supplemented by a more recent source: Paul R. and Anne H. Ehrlich's *The Population Explosion* (New York: Simon and Schuster, 1990). These authors state that world population doubled between 1950 the Earth's population will increase to between six and seven billion, and by the year 2100 to fifty billion, if the growth rate continues unrestrained. The human race is currently battling starvation. What would we do with a population of thirty to forty billion? It is quite unlikely that any foreseeable technology could save us.

At this writing the world's population is about five billion. Many regard this as a matter of grave concern. By the year 2050, the population could be seventeen billion or higher. These estimates are based on an annual population increment of two percent. What if the actual rate is twice that or even one-half that? It could be.

Suppose now that the calamity has arrived; that fifty percent of the Earth's population is starving; that food production is declining from overproduction, poor soil conservation, a failing technology, and other causes; and that transport of food is crippled by energy shortfalls. Suppose also that, despite everything, governments remain fairly well intact, which is not necessarily likely. What practical, feasible measures can be taken to rescue humankind from extinction?

Remember that no precedents exist for this situation. All proposed remedies will be untried, at least in this situation. Most of the wisdom of the past will be inapplicable. We cannot be our brother's keeper because we cannot even keep ourselves. New moral principles must develop from the realities of this particular human ecological crisis.

Food consumers are the only variable that can be manipulated. Food supplies cannot be increased. The inescapable moral conclusion is that food consumers must be radically reduced. Let us assume that fifty percent of the population will have to die to guarantee the survival of the species. In this instance, killing or dying by starvation are a toss-up since no humane method is available for doing either when such large numbers are involved.

Scenarios on this theme can be invented by the dozens. Perhaps some pockets of isolated populations would possess the resources to survive. All others would die. Assuming that reason and order prevailed, what are some additional survival strategies or moral principles that would have to be accepted and enforced?

---

and 1987 (p. 16); that the 1990 population of Earth is over 5.3 billion people and that 95 million more are being added yearly (p. 237). Between 1928 and 1990 the population of the United States rose from 120 million to 250 million (p. 13). No wonder automobile drivers are complaining about traffic congestion.

1. The use of every means of contraception including abstinence.
2. Abortion for all pregnant women for the duration of the crisis.
3. Infanticide.
4. Euthanasia of chronically disabled people of all ages.

All of the foregoing population reduction measures may have to be employed as a supplement to attrition from illness and starvation.

Measures mentioned to this point may prove inadequate if food production continues to decline in proportion to population growth. Such a circumstance may make emergency mass killings mandatory. Scientists in the field of human reproduction and world population research write scenarios of the aftermath of a population explosion more dismal than mine. One writer foresees the possibility that the last humans living on a sterile Earth will subsist during their final months by cannibalizing one another.

The foregoing excursion into catastrophic overpopulation provides the opportunity to observe some fundamental moral facts. I am convinced that it is morally lax to be unconcerned about population growth. Moral action can prevent as well as heal social crises. To the degree that we contribute to and address our disasters with irresponsible behavior, to that degree we must judge ourselves morally incompetent. The day is not far off when all forms of contraception and abortion will be recognized throughout the world as moral and legal.

The study of real and potential catastrophes brings us closer to the core of moral ecology. We have rather blithely plundered the natural environment. Now the world of nature is ready to strike back, injuring us severely. Our awareness of this situation is growing, but not nearly fast enough. Events of recent years are teaching us the reciprocity that exists between organism and habitat. *Our so-called habitat can do nicely without us, but we cannot survive without it.* We are at a point where a battered natural world is ready and capable of biting back. Even though the threat is of our making, we see it as coming at us from the outer environment. The moment of moral truth comes with the discovery that proper care of the natural environment is necessary and advantageous to our survival; that wise and loving care of our world is an ecological moral imperative.

It was once necessary and advantageous, and hence moral, for primitive humans to take from their surroundings all they needed and wanted. They were so few they hardly left a mark of their passing. They were, at most, minimal consumers. Evidence exists to show that in recent millennia, larger primitive populations in isolated regions such as New Zealand, did lasting damage to their environment by overutilizing and, thereby, exterminating some valuable species of animal life.

Today's human population is a gigantic consumer of natural resources; not enough of any desirable resource remains, whether essential or not, for all to have as much of anything as they might need or want. What was moral consumption in primitive times, would now be immoral, besides being an economic impossibility. Even the rich may soon be running out of things to buy. In many parts of the world people are too poor to even buy what they need, though what they consider necessities would not have been available to their primitive forebears.

In this comparison of primitive and modern humans, some essential facts show up. The constant or absolute factor in both situations is the critical matter of biological necessity and advantage. This is the arbiter of what is moral in both situations. All other factors are variables, brought on by supply and demand, which, in turn, is relative to another variable, population. The biological requirements of the human body, while flexible within narrow limits, do not change to accommodate the radical variables and exigencies generated by the environment. This is why I call organismic factors constants or absolutes.

If things we need are missing, we suffer. If we are beset by variables, we suffer. If we fail to cope with danger, we suffer. As organisms we must cope. The environment can mete out destruction, inconvenience us temporarily, and even satisfy our fondest hopes, but fundamental to the human species are our constant physiological and psychological needs, which, though rarely satisfied completely, are met well enough to keep us going.

It is this constant, invariable nature of biological realities that leads me to conclude all moral elements are absolute, not relative. A cursory comparison of the primitive and modern use of natural resources shows the former less capable of immoral overuse of resources, while the latter engages in wanton overexploitation of natural resources. When the environment bites back at humans, it is a signal that we are abusing it. This might beguile us into thinking that morality changes with population, thus suggesting that it is relative—a popular belief. Such a conclusion is in error because in an ecology of morals, the reference point, to which all other factors are relative, is the biological requisites of survival, from which moral elements derive.

One of the most difficult things for me to understand is why it was so hard for the leaders of the major world powers to proceed systematically and equitably to abolish the threat of nuclear war. It stuns the mind that so little has come of years of laborious negotiating. By now it should be clear to everyone that our failure to make our earthly home safe from nuclear destruction is a failure of moral competence. A thousand years ago a failure of this magnitude would have been called the work of the devil. An all-out nuclear exchange between the major powers, followed by nuclear winter, would not only produce the ultimate in immorality but the ultimate in unique situations. Humanity has no precedent for such a catastrophe and no certainty that even small, isolated groups would survive. Nuclear suicide of the human race would end everything including discussions about morality.

It seems to me that further elaborations of facts about nuclear dangers would, at this point, be redundant and add little or nothing to our understanding of morals. Further, the nuclear threat itself has been the most publicized human ecology subject in the media. While recent history witnessed unexpected political changes of great international significance, no guarantee against nuclear war has as yet been forthcoming.

Nuclear disarmament was embedded in a power struggle between the United States, the Soviet Union, and their respective allies. Before the accords of 1987, when one of the superpowers felt it was falling behind the other in some component of nuclear capacity, it started a catch-up construction program. Sensible or stupid, the constant jousting to keep ahead or catch up was euphemistically legitimized as fulfilling a need for parity and fairness. The real culprit is not nuclear war technology, it is the power struggle itself between two governments that supported two competitive political, cultural, and economic systems. Many small countries have been, and still are, developing nuclear weapons. For example, in 1991 Iraq, despite its defeat in the Persian Gulf War, was conspicuously attempting to produce nuclear capability. In the meantime we are left to wonder what political entities will control the nuclear arsenal of Soviet Russia in the year 2000. Future prospects are definitely not safe and sane. The immorality of the nuclear threat is still with us.

It is easy for us to recognize war in any form as a catastrophe. Wars begin with an offender or predator whose purpose is to use force and coercion to acquire superiority, profit, wealth, advantages, social control, cultural (perhaps religious) eminence, unquestioned leadership: in a word, power. Struggling for power and jockeying for controlling positions goes on in every walk of life: in family relations, in the scramble for job promotions, in labor-management contests, in politics, in business competition, in athletics, and so on. Other ingredients in this ferment are competitiveness and an adversarial climate that pervades practically all we do. I sometimes think these old behaviors—holdovers from ancient times—are gathering force and momentum and invite ever closer examination. They seem obsolete. They threaten a resurgence of barbarism. Perhaps they are harbingers of a collapse of our ecology, which would be a catastrophe.

A good illustration of the power factor in moral ecology is the almost universal hunger for upward social and economic mobility. We have serious doubts about the motives of people who want social dominance and control. In ancient times the rise of a dictatorial leader could have been adaptive and hence moral. Political dominance could be beneficent if the human ecological system at a particular time and place required it. The emergence of a strong leader could bring security to a tribal group who wanted it and would help work for it. Today, we have abundant evidence that a lust for power is pathological. With changing ecological conditions, many view a drive for power as a psychological disease that spawns catastrophes and most of the social, economic, and political ills of society. Certainly crime, as witnessed in the fierce competition of dope traffickers, is a catastrophic case in point. It is quite possible that the drive for power and control for the primary purpose of self-aggrandizement and serving the ends of special-interest groups is, in our time, reaching the limits of ecological tolerance. It is clear that Adolf Hitler's use of power was immoral and that the ecological damage of the Nazi movement is still a fact of life for millions. All power that is inimical to the biological welfare of humankind is immoral.

No article on the moral lessons of catastrophe would be complete without mention of two classical examples of moral dilemmas, both of which are rooted in catastrophe. They go under the names of "Triage" and "The Lifeboat Case."

Triage, after the French for sorting or selection, refers to the nighttime search of World War I battlefields for wounded American soldiers by teams of army nurses and medics. As each wounded soldier was found and examined, an on-the-spot estimate was made of his chance of survival. Those wounded who had a good chance of being saved were removed to a base hospital. The others, despite their pleading, were left to die. It must be recalled that large areas had to be searched under cover of darkness when enemy fire was at an ebb. The rescuers were small in number and had to work quickly. The deciding factor in triage was, "Who had the best chance of living?" This was an ecological decision based on biological constants: the conditions and requirements of living organisms. The rescuers could not save all the wounded. All could be left to die, or the more salvagable among them could be saved. Obviously, the moral way was triage (selection). Thousands were saved by this method. Morality was served, as well as possible, under the circumstances.

The scenario for the lifeboat case goes something like this: suppose an ocean liner is sinking. One-half the passengers and crew are in lifeboats pulling away from the sinking ship. The other half are in the water paddling with their life jackets on. Those in the water are heading for the boats and many are crying for help. If any of the unfortunates reach and board a lifeboat, the vessel will be swamped and sink under the stress of its many passengers. If this happened to all the lifeboats, all victims would be lost. What would you do if you were in charge of this situation? Order the lifeboats to pull away, which could conceivably save half the victims? Or, would you be guided by the tragic plight of those in the water? Those in the boats would stand the best chance of living. How would the practitioners of triage solve this moral dilemma?

In the next chapter I shall continue the theme of moral ecology, describing how modern technology has increased our awareness of the world around us, and showing how we have thereby become more integrated with our environment and how this modifies our perception of morality. Our survival as a species is at risk; if we don't care, who will? Certainly not nature. Even the mechanism of evolution is not programmed with any goal for us. So far as we know, the universe is neither moral nor immoral. It could continue on course without us. It may have to if we do not stop harming ourselves and our planet.

Francis Bacon, a founder of modern science, once said, "We cannot command nature without obeying her." If we want to survive, we must do what is necessary to attain this end. It is necessary that we care for our total environment. This means the proper care of ourselves, of others, and of the natural world, the three interdependent components of our environment.

16

Extending Our Environmental Reach

The life of an organism does not stop at its surface (for humans, the skin). It extends beyond this barrier and into the environment. A living organism is in continuous interaction with its environment. If our bodies were sealed from the environment, they would die in a matter of minutes. We see living organisms, then, as a part of the environment, not separate from it. Thus, in biology we must study the field of life, which consists of an organism plus its environment. This field theory is usually referred to as *ecology*. It is in this organismic-environmental field that morality develops as an offshoot of nature. This is why morality is not a mere whim or invention but a thing to be discovered somewhere in the interaction of our body-mind and its environment. This makes ecologically based moral elements a variety of natural law.

In Part Two I stressed that all moral principles come into being to bring about behavior designed to protect, preserve, and benefit our lives; that morals spring into being out of biological necessity. It is easy to grasp the connection between biological necessity and self defense, earning a livelihood, and protecting property, but less easy to understand how amusement, recreation, fulfilling desires, and appetites are offshoots of biological necessity. Nonetheless, they are. Take, for example, restorative recreations, the enjoyment of the products of human ingenuity, heating a home, or even having a telephone. Each can become a necessity. As we grow more dependent on the artifacts of civilization, a flu shot or a fast food joint becomes a necessity, not in a life and death sense, but in the sense of making life less stressful and more enjoyable. Life consists of a wide variety of experiences, some being more essential than others. And some experiences are utterly unnecessary, like smoking crack.

All of our sensory organs are means of extending ourselves into the environment. With touch, vision, hearing, sense of smell, and taste, together with the ability to walk, swim, and move about, primitive humans could probe and explore their habitats in search of the resources needed for sustaining life, for dangers against which they must protect themselves, for shelter, escape routes, and other essentials. Many activities, such as hunting and food gathering, are just as important to the human organism as such physiological processes as ingestion, digestion, extraction of nutrients, and elimination of wastes. Even during sleep, persons are in intimate contact with the supportive environment through the act of breathing. Modern humans are still at work on extending their knowledge and use of the environment.

Modern technology has consisted mainly of the invention and use of extensions of our organismic capabilities. Just a few of many examples follow:

- all our complex means of transportation and communication;
- all kinds of shelter, from grass huts to skyscrapers;
- synthetic fibers and plastic solids;
- instrumentation that boosts the capacity of biological structures, such as the hearing aid, electron microscope, prosthetic dental devices, and radio telescopes;
- medical treatment innovations, such as new drugs, nuclear medicine, dialysis machines, and artificial hearts;
- electronic science applications that extend brain capacity, nervous system sensitivity, and which may soon provide a super extension of our powers through artificial intelligence;
- nuclear power, space travel, and gene splicing.

These are all examples of humankind reaching out and are just a small representative sampling of the human ecological complex we have created. It is becoming problematic to describe where human biology ends and the natural environment begins; they have become so inextricably intertwined.

It is difficult to discern the boundaries between ourselves and the world around us. We are as deeply affected as our primitive ancestors by sunlight, darkness, air quality, wind, rain, storms, earthquakes, and everything nature can throw at us. We stand on our little Earth and look out at the universe and wonder what it is all about. Each of us has his or her own individual feelings about the mysteries out there. Utterly everything to which we react affects the biochemistry and physiology of our bodies. Each person interprets sensory input and develops concepts of the world that are neither exclusively a creation of mind nor a replication of the world. These interpretations are human impressions of the world that vary from person to person depending upon individual differences. Some individuals are colorblind, others not attuned to similar observational viewpoints. If this is a flaw, it is in the observer, not the environment.

This brings us to an important point. Morality does not exist anywhere in our natural environment or in any part of the universe so far as we know. Further, the natural world apparently has no feeling or concern for us. The only help it provides is what we wrest from it by our cleverness. The important point is that in the whole of the universe, the elements of morality can only be found in the interactions of human beings. Even Charles Darwin believed morality is a unique quality of humans. This makes morality a distinctly human characteristic. Just as humans exceed all other living creatures in intelligence, so do we exceed all other life forms in anything resembling moral behavior.

Morality is human. So is science. The American psychologist George Kelly liked to say that humans are natural-born scientists. They have been explorers, discoverers, experimenters, and problem solvers from the beginning. The scientific method was discovered little by little over the course of eons. We know the same is true of morals.

Humans, as scientists, have been around a long time. The discovery of such moral principles as caring, mutual protection, cooperation, and keeping agreements may be among the first scientific discoveries along with finding that a hunter's reach could be extended a long way with a spear. Moral law and science have developed side by side. Today, science and technology have presented us with new and as yet unsolved moral problems. These problems are of such magnitude and gravity as to make us wonder if humans, whether moralists or scientists, will be around for more than another century.

Extending our environmental reach through the scientific investigation of our Earth and the universe is harmless and, of course, moral. Scientific facts are incapable of doing direct harm to anyone. However, technology, the application of scientific facts and principles to the practical and industrial arts, can lead to both harmful and beneficial results for society.

We frequently hear of scientific and technological breakthroughs that are of tremendous benefit to humanity. It was not long ago that the World Health Organization announced that the scourge of smallpox had been wiped off the face of the earth. Significant breakthroughs are announced almost daily. However, these wonders do not inevitably lead to unmitigated blessings. People are beginning to awaken to the existence of the real harm of the greenhouse effect, a phenomenon that is primarily derived from burning fossil fuels in heating, in automobiles, and in electric power generation. Despite our love of warmth, cars, and electric power, love may turn to hate. The invention of the refrigerant gas freon has led to the first rupturing of the atmospheric ozone layer above the Earth. The ozone layer protects us from dangerous solar radiation. Freon gas escapes from junked refrigerators, automobiles, and is released by spray cans. It rises slowly into the upper atmosphere and chemically attacks the ozone layer. This illustrates how we can extend our environmental reach without any realization of the consequences. Of course, a few technological innovations do not have sad endings: water purification equipment makes our polluted water supplies safe, for instance, and the invention of the heart-lung machine has been a boon to hundreds of thousands. Capable technologies exist for the protection of our homes from fire and theft.

The primitive discovery that fire alleviated the pain of cold, aided in the preparation of food, and gave light and protection at night was a significant breakthrough. A body of lore for making and using fire continues to grow even today. The first use of fire led to immediate recognizable benefits. It is at the point of discovery how fire, for example, assists humankind in environmental adjustments that a moral element emerges and is recognized. In this case, human suffering and fear have been lessened and certain environmental threats reduced. Note that suffering and fear in this example represent the latent environmental impetus to act on behalf of the self. The discovery that fire ameliorates suffering and fear is a scientific finding. It is also an ecological moral finding because it preserves the self. It is rational to say that a moral finding is a scientific finding and *vice versa*.

A moral principle is a natural law that suggests what to do in a specific predicament where formerly, before the moral principle was discovered, we would have had to put up with, say, suffering and fear. In the example under discussion in connection with the use of fire, the moral principle says: "If you are suffering from cold, build a fire." A moral element is the evidence that a specific action meets the requirements demanded by a biological exigency (necessity, need, requirement, etc.).

Great benefits have come to humankind through the creation of our basic institutions, through arts and crafts, and, of course, through science and technology. It would take an encyclopedia to cover this giant topic. Suffice it to say that a shower of benefits and knowledge has been bestowed upon the human race from the time of the first written word to the time when researcher Jonas Salk discovered a vaccine for poliomyelitis. These benefits are statements of the moral orientation of humanity and we should be proud of them. But, when it comes to the technology of extending our employment of the natural biotic and abiotic environment, we have created some monsters that individually and, certainly taken collectively, could wipe us off the planet.

All the great innovative discoveries and inventions that extend and support biological structures and functions are followed by new or modified moral principles. Irrespective of when a moral principle is discovered, described, and conventionalized, whether it occurred in primitive or contemporary times, the conditions are identical. Each age produces new moral problems. For example, the surprise emergence of Acquired Immune Deficiency Syndrome (AIDS) has brought up new moral questions, and the rising tide of overpopulation may bring on many unpredictable moral problems. Needs and desires originate in the human biological structure (its ontology) and influences emanating from our environment. All must be met by appropriate, effective, and efficient behaviors. Moral science can be developed to deal with these aspects of our existence.

To cope with our environmental problems, we must rearrange some of our mental furniture. We might begin with the sacred cows, progress and growth. These are well-rooted popular concepts, the basic idea of which is going from something tolerably good to something better. Who needs such "progress" as urban sprawl, larger populations, and outgrown highway systems? A lot of investors and developers revel in population growth, but the majority of people are suffering from it. Progress as a concept is a myth scheduled for oblivion. We should not stop developers but we can control them by controlling population growth.

Another thing we must learn is that we do not need to use everything we invent. We do not need economic opportunism in the guise of new and better gadgets; hair, clothing, and decorative styles; cars; and the like.

The electronic revolution would not have been possible without super publicity and advertising. This revolution is not an unmitigated blessing either. My bank halts business when its computer breaks down. I sometimes wonder if we have not become too dependent on electronic gadgets. Arbitrage, a factor in the stock market crash of 1987 and a way of making money without producing goods or services, was one of the fruits of computer science. Of course, this form of immorality, discussed in a later chapter, is the fault of people, not machines.

A staggering obstacle to controlling technology is our slavery to it. We are addicted to our cars, televisions, household appliances, natural gas as well as gasoline, electricity, and so on. We are not only dependent on these technological marvels, we are eagerly looking forward to the promise of more to come. It is going to be hard for us to face the difficult road ahead, namely, the disappointments and sacrifices of living with the limitations imposed on us by our natural environment. Some will also feel disappointment and sacrifice imposed on them by fellow citizens. For example, how long must we put up with the immorality of manufacturing sports cars capable of speeds up to 125-mile-per-hour for operation by amateur drivers in bumper-to-bumper freeway traffic? This is the epitome of irresponsibility on the part of car designers, builders, buyers, state motor vehicle departments, law makers, and highway users.

Culprits in the misuse of technology are the human proclivities for competition and conflict. They are both adversarial, yet we cannot have one without the other. They can lead to harm or to benefit. They are among our less benign behaviors, rooted in biological law and the whole history of humanity. Both can be present in every activity from war to games to the marketplace. Competition and conflict must be among the most primitive of behaviors. Their employment on an enormous scale, as in the whole of the twentieth century, makes us question if the human race can ever really civilize itself.

A threat to a moral society and a humanely considerate use of technology is our fervor for a wide range of competitive and conflicting behaviors that are generally held in high regard in our society. A few of these are: our passionate pursuit of upward social and economic mobility; our lust for power, prestige, and wealth; our mad race to excel at any price; and our willingness to forgo long-term benefit for a short-term gain. These behaviors and objectives are often out of alignment with the concept that the pursuit of our personal interests and objectives best serves us when they also serve the welfare of others. Our culture has reached a stage that calls for a reassessment of the morality of our workaday customs, economic methods, aspirations, career models, and related factors. The time has arrived when we must adjust to the demanding requirements of producing and maintaining a livable human ecology.

In correcting environmental mistakes of the past and present, we must make a beginning somewhere. It seems to me that we must begin with the realization that our subject is a property that belongs to all of us: our natural biotic and abiotic world. Our first task would be to slow down and, if possible, ultimately halt the dispoilation of Earth. Population control is one means to this end. It will, no doubt, be unpopular, but it is inevitable at present rates of population increment. We have seriously overdrawn or overburdened every natural resource. No technological remedy is in sight. Primitive behavioral tendencies, backward notions of progress, success, and what I have called the morality maze have all contributed to our environmental problems.

This chapter has been, in part, a story of brilliant successes and hapless failures. The failures have to be corrected. Doing this is a biological necessity, an advantage, and a life enhancer: a necessity if we wish to survive, an advantage if we wish to realize our potential for self-mastery, and a life enhancer if we can also find fulfillment of our human aspirations.

17

Life Flow and Life Cycles

A bioenvironmental or ecological theory of morality has been introduced, a morality having its roots in biological necessity, advantage, and life enhancement. Central to this theory is the idea that our total organismic being belongs to us and is the instrument through and by means of which we experience the whole of life. We are the sole owner of this piece of property we call our body and mind.

To some people it may seem strange to think of one's body as a piece of property, over which one holds exclusive right. This has not been and may not always be true, for no natural law or right exists that guarantees us the ownership of ourselves and the possession of life. All levels of government in the United States are required by law to protect our lives. However, such laws will not protect us from drowning or being electrocuted by lightning—a reminder that no natural right to life exists.

Life is tenuous at best. We are compelled by the nature of things to accept our vulnerability to physical and mental injury as a natural part of existence. We are threatened daily by potential emotional stresses: e.g., the loss of a loved one, the loss of a job, being mugged or terrorized. We can be subject to automobile accidents, earthquakes, serious diseases, and other potential sources of death and injury. If we could not accept chance as a natural ingredient of life, our lives would be fear ridden and severely limited. One of the remarkable characteristics of human nature, born out by history, is our ability to cope with the exigencies of life. This is a part of the corpus of morality: to survive if at all possible.

Our bodies are an inheritance passed down to us through millions of years of evolution. Life is a continuous flow like a great river. We begin our introduction to the flow in the sexual union of a mother and father, thus bringing ova and sperm in favorable proximity for a sperm cell and ovum to unite. This union, if successful, produces a zygote, which is one more part in a continuing cycle progressing from embryo to fetus, then to infant, child, adolescent, adult, and, finally, to old age and death. Of course, for the human race as a whole, this flow has never been interrupted, but for an individual life the life cycle can be interrupted at any point by accident, malnutrition, disease, human causes, and by so-called natural death. We are all born to die. This is a fact of the individual life cycle. The enduring life flow is a fact of the whole of human existence.

The problem of when life begins is a purely human construction. Why should it take on an air of importance? The facts of biological life flow eliminate the problem of life's beginning and return it to the vagaries of evolution. The actual union of a sperm cell and ovum occupies a unique function in the flow of life, but it is of no more importance . . . nor less, in the life cycle than any other identifiable stage, such as first heart beat, birth, maturity, or death. The joining of a sperm and ovum is not the beginning of life, or a life, but a passing incident in the continuous flow of life. Life has no cessation or beginning. Spermatozoa and ova are life. They die by the trillions everyday, cut down in the process of eternal life flow. It is life flow that is continuous and absolute, not the individual life cycle. The importance of various junctures of an individual life cycle are set by humans and are subject to change and error, which will be shown as we proceed.

I shall move on to an examination of the moral implications of life flow and the life cycle. As we look for moral principles that can be applied in the solution of behavioral problems, we shall be gaining practice in using the facts and theory of moral ecology that have been presented up to this point. I plan to move toward these objectives by analyzing a series of moral questions fundamental to daily life.

People are generally interested in matters of life and death. The subject is a part of our daily information diet. The media is a constant reminder, reporting news of murders, accidents, disasters, terrorist acts, killing of the unborn, and so on, and, of course, the subject even occupies our recreational time through such entertainments as theater, detective stories, and western shootouts.

Life flow takes little notice of the fate of life cycles. Human population has continued to grow throughout the whole of history despite famines, plagues, wars, and natural disasters. During the twentieth century, population has soared astronomically. Between 1950 and 1987 the world's population doubled.* Yet during this century we have lost more people to wars than in all armed conflicts throughout history. Ninety million lives were lost in World War II alone, not counting civilian fatalities. Such evidence may indicate an inverse relationship between the growth of the river of life and the decline of the quality of life. As the life flow—the number of individuals in the life cycle—gathers force it pushes aside hoards of individuals as expendable excess baggage. Every age has had poverty and unemployment, but ours is the first to abet these scourges with rapid population and technological expansion. The need to control life flow is obvious. We must not wait until the doing of this becomes necessary. Population control is a moral imperative and its time has come.

It is interesting to note as we read on that life flow has seldom presented us with moral problems. Life-cycle phenomena have occupied the moral spotlight. We are approaching the time when life flow is beginning to change from moral neutrality to an environmental threat and a source of new and crucial moral problems.

The question as to whether life is highly valued is rarely raised. That life has great value seems to be taken for granted, yet history demonstrates that people have been killing one another as though the victims had no value. The reasons given for killing are as varied as the means employed. People have been killed because they did not believe in God, and because they did believe in God. In the Old Testament, God killed Onan for failing to obey a command. Little proof exists that humankind has placed great value on life: people fail to follow the advice of their doctors, risk their lives in certain sports and engage in the wholesale slaughter of wars, and many tend to deny vulnerability to risk—the "it won't happen to me" stance. Forty-five to fifty percent of the population are users and addicts of alcohol and drugs. While thousands commit suicide each year, millions of terminally ill or mentally ill people can hardly be expected to be overly enthusiastic about life. Before ending this sad recital, we would be remiss if we didn't mention the poor and unemployed among us. All these sufferers stand in great need of liberation from their sorry plight. Does the current cry to liberate the unborn prove that humanity is at last placing a more realistic value on life? Hardly. Preoccupation with the unborn, separated

---

*Paul R. Ehrlich and Anne H. Ehrlich, *The Population Explosion.*

from the ecological significance of the whole life cycle, may someday be regarded as pathological.

Nature does not seem to demonstrate that human life is precious either. Our built-in drive for self-preservation is often at odds with our propensity for multiplying our numbers and, consequently, our problems. But this was not always true. Primitive societies may have had too few children to maintain the optimum population of a social unit. Sometimes population growth may have exceeded available food supplies. In the United States today, we read almost daily of millions of homeless people. Children are frequently the hapless victims of unemployed and poor working parents. Millions of children receive the most meager care, physically and emotionally. Thousands are abandoned by their parents to live in the streets. In late 1988, newspapers reported the numbers of forsaken children as exceeding thirty thousand. If human life is precious, we should be tremendously concerned with the plight of so many endangered children. Instead, we hear of the overconcern of social and political leaders who focus on the moral problems of the beginnings of life, on the unborn and the medical anomalies of the newly born. These concerns may be taking precedence over the perennial moral problem of civilization: how to treat the whole of human existence as significant.

How dear is life? Are all stages of life of equal importance? Look at the evidence. In a single heterosexual union the male partner ejaculates upwards of sixty million sperm cells, only one of which may reach and fertilize an ovum.* All but one of the spermatozoa are superfluous and die, though they may have served an obscure biological function. But consider the sperm cells in the case of a male's nocturnal emissions, or semen produced by masturbation or ejaculation into a condom. All these life cells are lost. Should anyone care? Conversely, females ovulate monthly: over a lifetime a woman produces hundreds of egg cells or ova, most of which die unfertilized. All this potential life goes down the drain, so to speak. I have never heard or read any lamentations over this great loss of spermatozoa and ova. How dear is life at this stage of development? Is a fertilized egg cell (zygote) more important than an unfertilized ovum? If so, what causes the sudden increase in importance? How can the cause be identified?

The merging of a spermatozoa and an ovum is commonly, though inaccurately, regarded as the beginning of life. Life existed in these cells

---

*The Merck Manual of Diagnosis and Therapy, 14th ed., 1982, p. 1640.

before they joined and before the living cells were manufactured in the living bodies of the parents. Moreover, a means had to be provided for bringing the male and female life cells to proximity for joining, such as artificial or natural insemination. All this and more is a part of life flow, cycle after cycle. Singling out a point in an individual life cycle and setting it apart as the beginning of life reveals a lack of familiarity with human ecology and the biology of life flow. Further, if we see the movement from zygote to embryo to fetus to baby as possessing gradations of growing importance, this phenomenon of priority is something provided by our minds and not by nature, as we shall learn as the facts unfold.

Once the male and female procreative cells join and a viable zygote forms, a baby is definitely on the way. At this point in the life cycle a woman is not even aware that she is pregnant. Until the impregnated woman and others become aware that she is pregnant, no value is placed on the biological event that has taken place. Perhaps value is not an inherent quality of anything, but, like beauty, is in the eye and mind of the beholder. When a mother-to-be learns of her pregnancy, then a valuation of the new life takes form. She may experience joy or anxiety and despair, opt for a full-term pregnancy or choose to have an abortion.

At this point we may ask, is there a way to appraise the value of life at various stages in the life cycle? Is a zygote as significant as an embryo? Is the worth of a fetus based solely on the evaluation made by the mother and others? Does the mother have an inalienable right to terminate her pregnancy? Let us look at these problems through the lens of moral ecology.

We have at hand two simple but powerful ecological moral criteria: (1) that we own ourselves and (2) that we are responsible for coping effectively with our total environment. It is the fact that we own ourselves that lies behind the abolition of slavery, and it lies behind the judgment that a pregnant woman is not a slave to the new life in her uterus, but the reverse; she belongs to herself and the new life is a part of her. Neither anyone else nor the state has any claim to her primordial property. Any decision she makes regarding abortion is her constitutional right, a legal right, and is moral. As the sole proprietor of herself, she can decide whether she wishes to continue her pregnancy. A law or any societal stratagem that forced her to continue her pregnancy would be an infringement on her property rights. Worse, it would strip her of basic constitutional guarantees and make her a slave of the state for the duration of her pregnancy.

We have observed that many people hold that the significance of life varies during the life cycle. An individual spermatozoa or ovum has little significance. Nature allows them to die by the millions. However, as pregnancy moves on, stage by stage to parturition, a fetus steadily gains in worth and importance to parents, family, and society. While this does not always occur, the composite of varying individual valuations of stages of growth and development are all facts of nature, compelling us to examine carefully the whole process.

Is it moral to harm a fetus? The answer depends on the ecological context in which harm is done. Nature aborts fetuses and hence does harm. A study published in the *New England Journal of Medicine* (July 1988) and reported in *Newsweek* (August 15, 1988) reveals that 31 percent of all naturally implanted embryos miscarry, that 35 percent of all fertilized eggs never become live babies, and that one in four women reports awareness of having experienced a miscarriage. Commonly, these examples are referred to as spontaneous abortions. They naturally occur much more frequently than surgical abortions. The main ecological differences between spontaneous and surgical abortion is that the former is often seen as natural and unplanned, and the latter as artificial (contrived) and planned. It is hard to see how one can be preferred over the other by merely looking at the biological and environmental facts. In all cases harm has been done to the biological structures that make up the beginnings of the life cycle.

A new legal movement underway holds a woman responsible for injuring her fetus by, for example, ignoring her physician's instructions, using dangerous medications or recreational drugs, and by failing to protect and take care of her body. This movement goes under the rubric of "fetal rights." Spokespersons on all sides of this matter are emerging. In the future we may find ourselves with criminal laws and governmental agencies regulating and monitoring every moment of a woman's pregnancy and, in the bargain, perhaps requiring physicians to function as police. If this prospect were to be institutionalized, we shall be ready to take the next step and empower the state to raise "test tube babies" as in Aldous Huxley's *Brave New World*, which would put an end to biological motherhood altogether.

Simple alternatives to state regulation offer prenatal education, which could be incorporated in the family life education curriculum of public and private secondary schools, a premarital licensing examination on parenting and prenatal care, and greater attention by physicians to health and prenatal care education.

Fetal rights issues are collateral to the anti-abortion and right-to-life movements, both of which have been strongly supported by fundamentalist Christian religious sects, what was once called the Moral Majority, and the Reagan/Bush administrations among others. Whatever the source, the fetal rights issue is here. Can we believe that this issue evolved as an expression of love and concern for pregnant women and their fetuses, or as a distorted perception of morality? Actually, a fetus has no natural rights. Fetal rights, like any rights, have to be conferred by conventional law. If such laws are created, contrary to the primordial property rights of women, the right of females to choose to abort will be legally cancelled during pregnancy. Even a woman's body could be legally invaded by a surgical procedure to which she objected. Such laws, if passed, will expand the long list of immoral statutes.

The fetus is part of a pregnant woman's body and thus belongs to her. The moment it is born and is a viable infant capable of living independent of its mother's personal support, the infant belongs to itself. Parents or others who raise the child are the caretakers of the child, not the owners. The state may be concerned about fetuses, but should refrain from conferring rights upon them.

The pro-choice abortion argument advanced here rests in part on the following observations: (1) the mother is the sole owner of her primordial property and (2) this allows her the option to interrupt a pregnancy. Questions now arise regarding the status of a zygote, embryo, or fetus. Let us look into this matter in greater depth.*

At the onset we must acknowledge that the fetus is not an *integral part* of a pregnant woman's body in the sense of a major organ, such as the heart, liver, or lungs. The exit of a fetus by miscarriage, abortion, or normal birth would not doom a woman to death as would the loss of certain major organs. A fetus is more like a parasite than an actual part of a woman's body. At best, a fetus is but a temporary guest of a pregnant woman, be it welcome or not.

What is the property status of a zygote, an embryo, or a fetus? Our primordial property belongs to us, but what about the procreative lifeforms just mentioned? Do they belong to themselves or to the mother? Do they also belong to the father? In custodial contests between separated couples over so-called test tube babies, the father's claim is not for joint ownership of a frozen zygote or a viable infant, but merely for a permit to assume paternity and share responsibility for any offspring. (Again,

---

*See chapter 19, "Property, Profit and Morals," for a detailed discussion of primordial and material property.

we face the fact that no one owns a child, even a new-born babe. Parents and others may be caretakers, but not owners.) So, who owns it? I can find nothing in the life sciences to suggest that a father is co-owner of a fetus. Coercion of women to continue a pregnancy to term, whether it comes from the father, the state or other agencies, or individuals is immoral in the realm of moral ecology.

If it can be said that a mother owns the fetus and is, therefore, free to dispose of it like any other form of property, would it not be reasonable to also say that the fetus owns the mother? Probably we cannot go that far, but a good case can be built to characterize the mother as a total servant to the fetus and a slave to all who would regulate her pregnancy. A fetus does, in fact, draw its total subsistence and support from the mother. It shows no concern for the mother's primordial property, but takes from its mother whatever biochemicals it needs, irrespective of its mother's predicament or well-being. Setting aside time-honored sentiments concerning pregnancy and motherhood, it can be said that pregnancy, as a biological phenomenon, is a relationship of a determined parasitic growth and a willing or unwilling subservient host.

If a fetus is property, it is lacking in means of knowing it. A nonvolitional life form such as a fetus is a passive consumer. It produces no material property, and if it is itself property, it belongs to the mother. If it possesses legal rights, it is incapable of enforcing them. Fetal rights must be conferred and enforced by the state, which brings us back to law, politics, philosophical speculation, and religion, none of which necessarily reflect the laws of biological nature. Following genetic laws, a fetus spends its time developing as an organism. Beyond this biological drive, it cannot be described as being volitional. Being nonvolitional, it can own nothing, including itself. To own something one must lay claim to it and be able to enforce one's right to it. A fetus is utterly helpless, whereas a viable infant is not. Infants can live apart from their mothers. An infant's basic organ systems are, for the first time, all functioning as they will for the rest of the infant's life.

If we argue that a fetus owns itself and is, therefore, its own property, when does this transformation to property occur: at conception, at parturition, or in between? Such problems are reminiscent of the theological conundrum of ensoulment. These questions do not readily lend themselves to biological analysis and research. I believe we must, at least, tentatively conclude that the fetus, not being a volitional creature, is not physiologically ready to demonstrate or exercise the ownership of self. In other words, it is not yet a person among other persons.

The viable infant—the postnatal infant—is ready to be a person. It is one of us, which cannot be said of the zygote, embryo, or fetus except in a symbolic or sentimental sense. By the time of birth we have acquired a quota of genetic propensities that facilitate the learning of social behavior. Social learning, however, is not a conspicuous feature of uterine life. Learning how to be a human being begins at birth when the infant is introduced to the environment of others. I am not intimating that a fetus does not react in obscure ways to the life experiences of its mother. We know the fetus reacts to the neurohormonal gyrations of its mother and that she can pass on to the infant the handicaps of her lifestyle, such as drug abuse, malnutrition, and disease. Nevertheless, the differences of pre- and postnatal life are as striking as night and day. This rapid and permanent environmental shift has affected the personalities of us all. It is the beginning of learning about interpersonal relations and about property—both our own and that of others.

It may seem strange to mention property at this point; however, all interpersonal transactions involve property and all property involves people. This is a quirk of human ecology that has been virtually ignored by both the social sciences and moral philosophy. Now it comes up as the substantive beginning of moral development.

I support the view that a pregnant woman is free to function on a continuum of concern and care for her fetus, a continuum running all the way from zero to sacrificing her own life for the survival of her child-to-be. In our culture, people's affection and love for children extends to sentiments of caring for and protecting fetuses. However, the mother-to-be is not under any *obligation* to bear her child or to die for it. Nature places upon the mother the responsibility of carrying her fetus to term, but nature exacts no penalty for failing to do so. Nature allows us the freedom to control our lives and to control population. Both choices are moral.

Freedom of choice with respect to abortion is moral and should be legal. Those who choose abortion owe moral responsibilities to society. No matter where we stand on abortion, we must show respect toward those who believe differently. It will soon be generally conceded that world population must be controlled, or even turned back. Abortion may then be encouraged. Until such a time it may be wise to curtail abortion after, say, the twentieth week of pregnancy, except, of course, for medical emergencies. Advocates of free choice should conscientiously avoid unwanted or unplanned pregnancies. Women and men must observe that they do have at their disposal many safe and moral means of controlling procreation.

114 The Morality Maze

Democracy demands that all must be charitable in granting freedom of thought and action to one another, limited only by the avoidance of encroaching on the property rights of others. Government and the courts must not be beguiled by the notion that abortion is antilife.* We shall move on to a consideration of some reasons women give for deciding on an abortion.

When a woman exercises her primordial property rights by deciding to have an abortion, her decision is rarely based on trivial reasons. Often the reasons can be quite complicated and outside the scope of a "quick fix" through counseling. Some threats come from the outer environment of others: her mate may have deserted her, she is fearful of rejection by her friends and family, or her doctor warned her that a disease she has could be transferred to her baby. Other threats could come from the inner environment of her own mind: she feels incapable of supporting herself and a child, she hates the idea of giving up her baby for adoption, she has little confidence in becoming a good parent, or she does not want to bear the child of a rapist. Some pregnant girls and women are almost totally lacking in the requisites of successful motherhood. A culture could benefit by encouraging such women to have an abortion. It is possible that a sane and timely interception of a life cycle can be used creatively for the benefit of society and for the flow of life.

Suppose that an antiabortion amendment is written into the Constitution of the United States. How could it be enforced? If it were to meet the same fate as Prohibition, then enforcement would be difficult indeed. The Volstead Act resulted in a Constitutional amendment outlawing the manufacture and sale of alcoholic beverages in the United States. Its legacy was lawlessness, gangsterism, and the degradation of respect for constitutional government. This amendment was rescinded after doing considerable social and political damage to our country. Have we any evidence that the abolition of abortion and the conferring of fetal rights will be a less disastrous adventure than the prohibition of alcohol? Such laws will be impossible to enforce, and their costs will be staggering. This maneuver could conceivably lead to an Orwellian nightmare and the degeneration of our democratic society. Why should we not continue to put our trust in the democratic principles as set forth in the Constitution and allow women to choose whether to have an abortion according to their rights, their consciences, and their religious beliefs?

---

*Nonetheless the upset and fervor of the right-to-life advocates can be understood if we assume that life begins with the zygote and that the zygote and subsequently the fetus owns itself.

I have argued that a woman's ownership of her primordial property, which includes a possible zygote, embryo, or fetus, may morally elect abortion and that any interference with this right destroys her status as a free individual. But, having said this, under what circumstances can abortions be moral or immoral? We might start with the fact that nature neither requires nor forbids abortion. Millions of spontaneous abortions (miscarriages) occur every year. This seems to say that nature condones abortion. Likewise, millions of induced and surgical abortions occur every year. This is condoned legally in the United States, though a politically powerful segment of the population believes that abortion is immoral; that it is an actual killing of babies even though what is destroyed is an embryo or early stage fetus, not a viable baby. The emotional impact of the thought of killing babies by abortion clouds a rational approach to find solutions for the moral dilemmas posed by abortion. Let us examine the problem from a different angle, from the viewpoint of torturing fetuses rather than killing them outright.

Medical technology can now sustain the lives of premature babies born after twenty-four weeks. Only about 5 to 20 percent of these babies make it to childhood. In the neonatal care process, they are wired to instrumentation and their every physiological process is meticulously monitored. They are hooked up intravenously to medical and nutritional supplies, their lungs are ventilated by special equipment, and they live in an environment that is tortuous compared to that of a mother's uterus.

Is such a neonatal medical program on a different moral plane than abortion? We have determined that in an ecologically moral system, abortion, which terminates a life cycle, is moral. Care of premature babies, so small they can be cradled in the palm of the hand, forecasts uncertain results, the probable suffering of the infants, and enormous financial costs. One course of action eliminates an unwanted pregnancy, the other extends the life of some babies to fulfill a federal regulation that demands treatment for all viable fetuses no matter how prematurely born. If both courses of action were abandoned, life flow—the most important biological fact of species survival—would go on as usual. Millions of life cycles begin and end every day. Life flow has no discernible natural beginning or ending. In solving reproductive moral problems, we must recognize and adjust our thinking to the ecological importance of life flow. Preservation of this flow is a biological necessity. We fulfill this necessity quite well, judging by the rapidly expanding world population. The realities of life flow put to rest the question of when life begins or when it ends, for that matter.

Let us return briefly to the neonatal account for a few additional facts. The percentage of premature infants who live increases with the fetal age at the time of birth. The medical management of preemies born between 24 and 35 weeks of pregnancy requires extremely complex and labor-intensive care. Even in the country's best hospital intensive care nurseries, many of these infants have a low survival rate. Also, those who do survive have more physical and mental abnormalities by the time they reach childhood than children who were carried to the full term of pregnancy.*

Is such aggressive medical treatment of preemies born during the 24th to 35th week of pregnancy moral, considering that their chances of living a normal life are slim? The medical treatment of viable infants of this class is certainly moral, but the matter of its importance and desirability is debatable. For example, the costs of the high levels of medical skill and technology required are so high ($350,000 per infant) that we wonder if the talent, effort, and money used could be more advantageously employed in researching and improving prenatal care. The latter course would ultimately reduce or, probably, eliminate the need for treating very premature infants. We also wonder why the federal government is urgently pushing neonatal medicine while more mature citizens need greater protection from disease, traffic deaths and injuries, poverty, homelessness, and unemployment.

What is it that befogs our moral perceptions? The answer to this question is buried in the tangle of the morality maze: conflicting folkways, customs, conventions, political motives, laws, religious doctrines, and prejudices. People will ultimately have to rise to the exigencies of overpopulation. They will then employ all means of procreation control, such as abstinence, diaphragms, condoms, sterilization, surgical abortion, and biochemical methods of contraception and abortion. We shall conclude that all are moral if safe and effective medically. None will be regarded as morally superior to another. Some will of course receive lower marks medically than others. Abortion is probably one of these. Since live births occur after twenty-four weeks of pregnancy, we may, at this time in history, want to restrict or disallow abortion after the twenty-fourth week of pregnancy. This last statement is an example of the modification of a moral entity by ecological factors, in this case, the discovery of new neonatal medical facts. If world population were to double or triple by 2050, all reproductive morals would be changed drastically to meet the biological

---

Newsweek (May 16, 1988).

requirements of an ecosystem crisis. This type of crisis was discussed in chapter 15 on "The Moral Lessons of Catastrophes."

The values we learn to place on pregnancy and babies in our culture are the result of a complex social and psychological process that begins in our own babyhood and continues throughout all subsequent stages of our personal development. No two people pass through exactly the same family life situations and community learning experiences, nor do they arrive at the threshold of parenting equipped with a similar mix of traits, attitudes, emotional responses, and knowledge respecting the start-up phase of parenting, which coincides with the day the prospective mother learns she is pregnant. When the female partner knows she is pregnant, the parents-to-be may enthusiastically place a positive value on their greatly desired child-in-the-making. As time goes on, the fetus becomes of great concern and value to the prospective mother, father, and grandparents, as well as other relatives and friends.

The importance of all life is derived from how we perceive it, and a fetus is no exception. It has no intrinsic, understandable worth aside from that placed on it by its parents and other concerned persons. It usually picks up importance as its birth approaches: preparations for the birth of the baby accelerate and names are discussed. More people become involved: the mother's physician, the hospital, and suppliers of baby paraphernalia. Perhaps a party or shower is given for the expectant mother.

After the baby is born, society assumes responsibilities, such as the safety, health, and education of the child. By the time a child arrives at adulthood, society and the parents have made a tremendous investment in its development: not only money but love and psychological support. By this time we have been beguiled into thinking that the importance of the fetus has increased manyfold. This leads to the illusion that the value of a life varies during its maturation. All stages of the life cycle are a creation of nature and nature does not indicate that one stage is more important than another.

THE MORAL DILEMMAS OF MODERN MEDICINE

Three out of every one hundred children are born with congenital defects. Quite often such children are liabilities to parents and society. These are the medical anomalies we have all read about or have seen on television;

the child born without an immune system, with a brain stem but no brain, with other serious anatomical defects, or with handicapping mental as well as physical deficiencies. Advances in medical science and technology are successfully rescuing some of these children. In the most hopeless examples, death may be preferable to life. Just a hundred years ago, children in this classification were not kept alive at all costs. Basically, two reasons were given for this: (1) the medical technology to keep such medical cases alive had not yet been invented and (2) parents and society had no strong motivation to keep them alive, primarily because neither group was prepared emotionally, socially, or economically to cope with burdensome children.

Infants born with medical anomalies have been common throughout human history. Equally common was the putting to death of such infants. The ancient Greeks practiced infanticide as a matter of course. The practice was regarded as both legal and moral: their religious view was that the body was the temple of the soul, and they reasoned that if the body of a newly born babe was defective, so was its soul and, therefore, it should be destroyed. This was a simple solution to an everyday problem and seemed to be a generally acceptable practice for centuries. Until quite recent times newly born infants who were adjudged defective were smothered or causally allowed to die from starvation (though hydration and pain medication kept the infants comfortable). The less seriously disordered died during childhood; still others became wards of state or private hospitals for their lifetimes.

Technology has created other moral dilemmas. During pregnancy a grown woman was accidentally brain damaged. She never regained consciousness. She was kept alive in a hospital by life support technology until the baby was born and viable. This incidence points out that a mother, reduced to negative status, acquired near zero value. Her baby advanced from a secondary value to a primary value when it was determined that its mother stood no chance of recovering. Every professional, legal, and lay decision throughout this case was moral. The baby was saved without diminishing the mother's primordial rights whatsoever. Certainly, saving the fetus from the threat posed by the mother's imminent death was moral.

The reverse of the case just cited is that a pregnant woman's life may be saved at the cost of her fetus's life. This is based on a kind of folk wisdom, according to which a woman's life is worth more than that of her fetus. This is not only an example of moral killing, but it illustrates that the value placed on human life is generally perceived in our culture as increasing with age until full organismic maturation of powers has been attained.

Advances in medical technology have created baffling new moral dilemmas: Who is entitled to the limited availability of heart and other organ transplants? How should limited resources, such as dialysis machines be fairly dispensed? How much of the resources of a technologically advanced hospital and staff should be allocated to the treatment of rare medical anomalies? These are just a few of the many questions facing us each day. The search for answers has generated new fields of paramedical specialties like bioethics and forensic medicine. Attorneys, the courts, and state legislatures are now deeply in the fray creating as many moral problems as solutions. Old laws receive new interpretations, new laws are hammered out in state legislatures, and courts are harried with questions of surrogate mothering (Baby M and Baby Doe) and the ethics of the AIDS epidemic. We have come face to face with our ignorance of morality and how we frequently confuse moral issues with emotions, religious concepts, law, and politics.

We search vainly for original moral problems in the hullabaloo over modern medical technology and practice. For example, take the life-and-death matter of "pulling the plug," a lay phrase that refers to removing life support systems. Physicians know that without such support their patients will die in a matter of days. We cannot, as a rule, blame physicians for wanting to keep patients alive. Saving lives is their business. A time is reached, however, when it becomes futile to keep patients alive by purely artificial means. When physicians, their co-workers, and the patients' families and/or legal guardians know this, a simple legal step can be taken to effect the cessation of treatment. Quite often patients are aware and approve of what is being done and why. The interruption of life support efforts ironically can be interpreted as legal and moral killing. It also can be thought of as a loving release from life.

A second example of a moral problem is the surrogate mother: a woman who agrees to bear a child for another woman who, for one reason or another, cannot bear a child of her own. No basis can be found in moral ecology for regarding surrogate motherhood as immoral, even though the mothers themselves can act immorally. It might be mentioned that parties to the agreement can fail to keep their contracts. The following true story concerns a surrogate mother who bore a viable baby for a contracting couple but refused to give up the baby according to the terms of the contract. Her excuse was that mother love would not permit her to relinquish her baby. The surrogate understood that this was one price all contracting surrogates must expect to pay. Every day many women lose babies from disease, street accidents, and the like. These women do not use this insult to their mother love as an excuse to dissolve relationships or break contractual obligations. Compassion for the surrogate mother in my story became a factor in the case and it was not cancelled out by popular lay compassion for the disappointed couple who, after months of waiting and emotional preparation, were cheated in the end by a fraudulent surrogate. Courts, law, and compassion are poor substitutes for morality. A surrogate mother does not own her child anymore than any other parent. The courts and law should recognize the moral facts of ownership and primordial property.

SEX DRIVE

The human endowment of a powerful sex drive is a major component of our procreative capacities, which, together with our drive to survive, our superior intelligence, and our propensity for loving and bonding constitute the generative forces of life flow. All our reproductive functions and capacities are essential to our existence.

In a biological sense, it is absurd to view sex as other than moral. If we regard sex as less than moral, then logic demands that we judge the procreative process and the resulting life flow as something other than moral rather than as a miraculous triumph of nature.

Among possibly hundreds of monosexual, homosexual, and heterosexual practices, some may be illegal and others condemned on religious grounds, but none would be classified as immoral in an ecology of morals. No sexual behavior in, of, and by itself is immoral. For example, no such thing as a sexual crime or immorality exists, but crimes and immoral acts include sexual behavior. So there we have it. Sex, in any form, is moral. We have no sex crimes, but we have crimes involving sex, which will be analyzed shortly.

Sexual behavior is of much concern in everyday life. In religion, law, and social convention, heterosexual behavior has been taken as a norm or standard prescribed by nature or God as a means of procreation. That heterosexual activity was made appealing and pleasurable is regarded as nature's way of insuring that copulation and reproduction would take place. Deviations from heterosexual copulatory behavior were viewed as substitutive, compensatory, inferior, sinful, immoral, or illegal, depending on the specifics of the sexual act, and environmental factors such as time, place, and so on.

Sex and Crime

All crimes involve property, and so-called sex crimes are no exception. Rape is one of the best known and most despicable of all crimes. Consider what is involved in rape. In the classical sense rape is a sex act forced on a male or female victim against the victim's will, choice, or consent. Threats, coercion, or force by the rapist are common features of rape. These actions fall uninvited upon the victim and constitute an assault on the victim's primordial property. As a result, rape victims may lose their lives, be robbed of other personal property, and/or sustain temporary or permanent physical and psychological damage.

Rape may be defined as the destruction or usurpation of another's right to the control of his or her property. This is what makes rape immoral, not the sexual component. In describing the rapist we must look beyond sex drive for the crucial motivators of rape. No proof is available that sex drive alone inspires rape. This fits the definition that no immoral act is motivated by biological necessity. Also, the rapist is not motivated by environmental threats, but is the threat himself. Thus, we have analyzed the criminal and immoral components of rape without describing the coincidental sexual components that are basically irrelevant morally. This could mean that the sexual history of rape victims need no longer be considered pertinent to the moral and legal status of victims. Laws should be changed to recognize these facts.

The moral factors uncovered in the foregoing analysis of rape can be applied to all so-called sex crimes. Sodomy (penile-anal intercourse) between consenting adults is moral, however, prison gang rapes of young men in which the latter are forcibly sodomized is immoral. Again, the rape victim's primordial property rights are violated: he is humiliated, exploited, brutalized, and frequently wounded despite his protests and resistance. All the components of immorality are present: the rapist gang does not sodomize out of biological necessity, and the gang itself represents the threat. The prison gang asserts power over the lives of weaker victims. These are the very immoral and criminal behaviors for which the gang members were imprisoned. We may be sorely tempted to recommend that such inveterate offenders be separated permanently, even from prison society.

Officials of the University of California at Berkeley condemned the prevalence of a student practice called "date or acquaintance rape" (*San Francisco Chronicle*, January 23, 1987).This is the sexual rape of women student acquaintances through intimidation or coercion. "Date rape" was declared an unacceptable behavior thought to be a widespread social problem affecting almost every student on all college campuses. Male students behave as though the victim exists for their pleasure. Seemingly the young men have not been taught that women have primordial property rights: rights to refuse sex, and to decide when, where, and with whom they will have sex, if at all. Such immoral behavior on the part of male college students suggests that our society is incompetent in basic moral education.

I shall not go into the details of every sexual practice. Such an excursion would add little to our knowledge of sex-related morality. Suffice it to repeat the basic moral statement that no sexual behaviors are inherently immoral or injurious. The immorality and injury stem from related behaviors that are not sexual. Sex crimes always involve force, injury, coercion, intimidation, cajolery, fraud, brutality, and murder, all of which are forms of immorality. Knowingly transmitting a sexual disease would be an example of injury. An unfulfilled promise for sexual favors would be an example of fraud. A moral person would never cause any individual to participate in a sexual act that is unwelcome, distasteful, or injurious. This rule applies to all sexual behaviors involving heterosexuals and homosexuals, and includes married couples. What follows are some special examples of sex-related activities that require a few additional words.

Sexually Transmitted Diseases

More than twenty modern Sexually Transmitted Diseases (STDs)—formerly known as Venereal Diseases—like all infectious diseases, are injurious if not deadly. The best known STDs are gonorrhea, syphilis, genital herpes, chalamydia, and Acquired Immune Deficiency Syndrome (AIDS). To be the innocent victim of an STD, say, through a blood transfusion, is no more immoral than being the innocent victim of an automobile accident. The mounting battle against STDs may have the side effect of raising our awareness of our personal biosocial responsibility with respect to protecting ourselves and others against all infectious diseases. Many people already stay home from work when they are feverish or are obviously coming down with an infectious illness. It is easy to understand that to knowingly transmit deadly AIDS is equivalent to murder or the crime of a roadside sniper. No age group escapes the ravages of STDs: children are frequent victims of these diseases, acquiring them primarily from their mothers, particularly during birth.

AIDS can teach us a great deal about the ecology of morals. It is incurable at this writing; no preventative vaccine has been discovered, and it is easily transmitted via body fluids. Infected people may carry the disease for years before developing symptoms, but during this time they can infect others. It is deadly, spreading rapidly, and must be slowed and eventually stopped. It is a threat to the human race as a whole and any effective, rational means of combatting it is moral. If the disease continues to proliferate, I predict that, among the many preventative and precautionary measures that will be taken, the following will appear:

1. AIDS victims and carriers who knowingly infect others will be treated as murderers.
2. AIDS victims will be quarantined for the remainder of their lives.
3. The total population will be tested for AIDS antibodies and the information obtained will not be regarded as confidential.
4. The right to privacy will be temporarily rescinded.

All of these measures will be regarded as moral because they are derivatives of biological necessity. Any behavior or discovery that assists in turning back the AIDS tidal wave will be regarded as moral. We are all here because our survival drives have top priority.

Prostitution

It is common in our society to earn a living by selling products, ideas, and services. The prostitute, female or male, is no exception. Prostitutes do not force their sexual services on anyone. If they avoid spreading STDs and do not engage in immoral sidelines, such as robbery and blackmailing, their services are as moral as any other personal service for hire. Yet, prostitution is illegal and considered a criminal activity, even though the so-called crime is victimless. The rising public consciousness of the dangers of promiscuous sex may put the world's oldest business out of business. It's happened before. The Old Testament reveals that venereal disease was rampant in the ancient world. Since these times religions have regarded prostitution as immoral and sinful. If modern prostitution proves itself to be a menace to public health, it will once again be regarded as immoral and this time in the frame of moral ecology.

Childhood Sex and Morality

Sexual curiosity and experimentation among children seems to be normal in most societies and no substantial data indicates that this does psychological damage. Adults frequently catch children at sex play and scold and punish them for wrongdoing. This may initiate anxiety about sex that is more harmful, psychologically, than the sex play alone ever could be.

The sexual molestation of children by adults is another matter, however. It is difficult, if not impossible, for children to understand and adjust emotionally to the sexual advances and erotic behaviors of adults and sexually sophisticated adolescents. Plenty of psychiatric evidence indicates that such encounters interfere with the child's social development and emotional well-being. The problems of sexual and emotional adjustment may carry over from childhood into adulthood. Children are not ready experientially, nor are they strong enough, to protect themselves from sexual exploitation by adults. In fact, young children may not even be aware that they are being misused or harmed in any way. The sexual abuse of children is an environmental threat with which they are unprepared to cope. The abuser is not motivated by biological necessity and is invading the primordial property rights of a defenseless child. Either or both of these criteria define the abuser's behavior as immoral.

Teenage Pregnancy

Modern American urban society has no established, unified ecosystem. No generally accepted rules govern child-bearing by immature parents, or socially and economically incompetent parents of any age. Our population is a mix of racial stocks, nationalities, religions, behavioral standards, learned and ignorant people, affluent and poor people, as well as the bright and the dull. We are a nation without a common, agreed upon moral code. We are held together by an almost blind faith in our democratic, constitutional form of government, and we do not know what to do about the rising tide of teenage pregnancy.

In the primitive Polynesian society described by anthropologist Margaret Mead in *Coming of Age in Samoa*,* children were raised to regard sex as a natural process, like sleeping. Sex was disassociated from taboos, fears, and wrongdoing. The body did not need to be clothed for the sake

---

*Pp. 201ff. of chapter 13. This source provides a detailed comparison of Samoan and American sex and family customs.

of modesty, and the institution of marriage was not as formal and binding as we attempt to make it. Sex was as casual as eating a meal. If a teenager became pregnant, her elders and age mates would likely be accepting. When the baby arrived, it would be welcomed and cared for by all. Mead described a human ecological system that worked for a tribe of Polynesians.

We are almost as permissive about sex behavior as Mead's Polynesians, but the similarity ends there. The plain fact is that society does not want or need the babies, the attendant costs, or the social deterioration. Even if we knew what to do about teenage pregnancy, no person or agency in our society has the power or authority to do something about it. Parents of teenagers, the schools, religious organizations, and governments at all levels are helpless. The most powerful nation on earth, which we enjoy calling ourselves, is unable to cope with its sexually active teenagers.

The Polynesians had a simple life: an abundant food supply free for the taking, a few village chores, no crime as we know it, some practical rules of conduct, and a well-ordered social life. All tribal members participated in the care and rearing of children. When Mead's study was made, these people were living in a down-to-earth, simple society. Children running around and babies being born were part of the enjoyment of life. Further, it was their custom for females to bear children from first menstruation on, and teenage girls knew all they needed to know about life and mothering.

By contrast, we live in a confusingly complex society. Hardly anyone at any age knows all they need to know to get by. We need lifelong involvement in education. We use the services of hundreds of specialized businesses, trades, and professions. We are not born learned and wise. It takes great effort and discipline just to learn enough to be self-sufficient economically let alone to achieve wisdom. Often our teenagers just do not have what it takes to be parents. The vast majority are dependents, lacking in job skills, barely literate, emotionally unstable, and hardly qualified to make such an important decision as to have or not to have a child. Worse yet, we have failed to give them the background to thread the morality maze of teenage pregnancy.

We must teach children the truth about the morality of sex. Sex in and of itself is moral. What is immoral is indulgence in sexual activity without regard for the related responsibilities. For example, teenage pregnancy is not just a prank or a careless mistake that can easily be lived down. It may be a devastating form of long-term harm to self, to one's sex partner, to one's parents, and an unwelcome burden to society.

Most of the nation's public secondary schools offer instruction in sex education, teaching the biological facts of sex and the basics of sexual hygiene and contraception. Many schools are still squeamish when it comes to teaching about eroticism and the full range of psychosocial sexual behaviors. Still fewer high schools provide such student services as sex clinics and sex counseling. Much of this is changing as a result of the AIDS epidemic of the 1980s.

Despite all these innovative sex instruction and information programs, teenage pregnancy rates are not declining. Something is missing. Perhaps it is moral education. Educators know a lot about the process of moral development and how to teach morals. The trouble seems to be muddled ideas and thinking about morality. The consequence of this is that teachers are not certain about what moral principles to believe and to teach. No matter what moral position is taken in sex education, there will be some vigorous community opposition to it.

Consider for a moment the most important biological fact of human sexual reproduction: a newborn infant, a new member of the human family. This is the stage in the life cycle to begin the analysis of the morality of pregnancy and to inquire into the subject of respect for life.

It is important for everyone, not just teenagers, to learn that under certain circumstances pregnancy is a form of immorality. It is immoral if it results in a culturally deprived and disadvantaged child, if the lives of the young parents are stunted by burdens and responsibilities for which they are totally unprepared, and if the teenagers' parents are saddled with tasks and expenses that diminish the quality of their lives.

Adolescents should not be taught that "respect for life" denies them an escape from pregnancy through abortion. It is a travesty that respect for an embryo or fetus supercedes respect for a pregnant girl who does not want to have a baby. Further, teenagers should be taught that respect for life is not demonstrated by refraining from the use of contraceptives, but by refraining from producing a child before the sexual partners are ready.

Somewhere in the high school sex and family life curriculum the responsibilities of motherhood, fatherhood, and parenting should be taught. The importance of learning about the exacting and awesome occupation of effective parenting should be placed ahead of sex instruction. I see this as a base for inculcating motives for avoiding pregnancy during adolescence, and as raising the significance of a unit of instruction on contraception.

All human societies have been driven by dire circumstances to regulate sexual behavior. The targets of regulations have often been sex acts themselves as well as sex-related behaviors, such as fighting over mates, adultery, rape, polygamy, child abuse, promiscuity, virginity, and so on. The institution of marriage was a life-saving practice and an aid to child-rearing. Monogamy was a health practice: the ancients were convinced that certain sicknesses were suppressed by virginity before marriage and monogamy afterwards.

Sex regulation was contrived as a protection from injury and social turmoil. Sexual taboos and prohibitions were frequently enforced by cruel punishments, even death. All religions have attempted to define a peaceful and orderly way of life that included the regulation of sex from the cradle to the grave. This was certainly true of Christianity. To this day established and prestigious religions have a body of doctrinal law that attempts to regulate the sexual practices of members. Those who disobey religious sexual prohibitions are regarded as sinners who must seek some sort of atonement for their transgressions.

Our free and open society may one day find teenage pregnancy and the pregnancies of certain other socially and economically incompetent sex partners to be immoral. When that happens, laws defining who will be licensed to bear and raise children will not be far away. The strict regulation of child-bearing is practiced in China today to control population growth, to enhance the quality of child-rearing, and to control distribution of social and economic resources. The Chinese are making it work. If they can, so can we. In fact, we may have no alternative in the near future.

FETAL TISSUE RESEARCH

In 1984, a Christian news organ known as *Biblical Scoreboard* alerted its readers to the start up of medical research employing fetal tissues acquired from aborted fetuses. Following this, many news articles on the subject have been published. By the end of 1988 it became apparent that the collection and sale of fetal tissue derived from abortions and miscarriages was to become a new research and business field capable of major expansion.

In November 1988, surgeons at the Colorado Health Science Center, University of Colorado, made the first transplant of fetal tissues into the brain of a man with Parkinson's disease.* The National Institute of Health

---

*Monitor, American Psychological Association (February 1989).

gave 116 grants for research using fetal tissue during 1987. Gifts of fetal tissue, administered under the Uniform Anatomical Gift Act, had been donated by mothers. Use of fetal tissue from induced abortions has been outlawed by eight states (at this writing). According to the APA *Monitor*, information on fetal tissue experiments can be traced back to the mid-1960s. Controversy emerging from fetal tissue use is greatest concerning fetal tissue supplies obtained through induced abortions. Opposition comes mainly from antiabortionists.

Biological materials derived from fetuses can probably be used in the treatment of a variety of diseases, such as Parkinson's, Alzheimer's, diabetes, and radiation sickness, to mention a few of dozens of possibilities. Also, it has been found that fetal body parts can be used in surgical transplanting. Further, women may come forward who are willing to rent their uteruses for the commercial production of fetuses scheduled for abortion during the mid-trimester of pregnancy. It is a strange new twist of fate that tissues from the earliest stages of life may be used to restore the health of older generations of humans. This new area of medical science and practice will, if it has not already done so, raise a storm of moral controversy.

On the issue at hand, the split of pros and cons approximates the well established split of pro-lifers and those who advocate freedom of choice. The pro-lifers cry "baby killers" and call the new enterprise an "obscene harvest." They also predict the ultimate reduction of life to a collective reservoir of biological materials to be used and manipulated in every conceivable way. Accompanying these thoughts is the intimation that we will ultimately consider drawing body parts and tissues from hopelessly defective infants, children, adults, and aged "vegetables."

Out there in the wide world are millions waiting for transplantable parts and new treatment procedures. They are the potential customers for the budding biological materials businesses. At least a million victims of Parkinson's disease are awaiting a miracle. Most could, chances are, benefit from biochemicals derived from fetuses. The medical demand for body parts and tissues outstrips the supply and will continue to do so even if all suitable fetal material is made available.

It can be argued that society will benefit from all these innovative procedures and from biomedical resources development by utilizing for human betterment otherwise wasted human tissue in the form of aborted fetuses. The benefits envisioned are significant new additions to the medical arsenal of life extension techniques. We must keep in mind that life extension is, after all, the primary function of the medical profession.

Life Flow and Life Cycles 129

At this point, we have become acquainted with many important principles of a theory of morals based on human ecology, and we are cognizant that such a body of theory does not necessarily lead to moral judgments that are aligned with certain established customs, religious doctrines, and civil laws. In the light of what we have learned, let us look closely at two controversial areas of moral problems growing out of human reproductive biology. They are identified in the following questions:

1. Should fetuses be used in biomedical research and practice?
2. Should we use and expand technologies designed to surmount fertility problems, e.g., sperm banks, "test tube babies," surrogate mothers, and artificial insemination?

Response to Question 1: No discernible harm or immorality takes place when experimenting with the tissues of a dead fetus. However, considering the current state of human ecology, it would be hard to justify such experimenting as necessary to the preservation of life-flow, though it is possible that such research could lead to new knowledge and medical therapies. The last matter has yet to be proved. Is it necessary to perform neonatal care on viable babies born between 24 and 35 weeks of pregnancy? For human ecological reasons, no. The biological flow of life will continue to flourish without this very early neonatal lifesaving drama. Is any biological necessity served thereby, or are we serving a misconceived administrative law?

Response to Question 2: It should be clear that our foremost responsibility and priority as a species is to protect our commonly shared natural environment. In chapter 15 we learned that we have already burdened our environment beyond its capacity to support us in health and well-being. No matter what we do technologically to rescue our habitat from further destruction, we must resign ourselves to the unwelcome and inevitable task of worldwide population reduction and control. I must emphasize again that this is a moral imperative and we must not allow it to be sidetracked by other important objectives.

The tide of human life flow is increasing rapidly. It does not require further stimulation. Human ecology events force us to conclude that progenerative technologies are no longer needed, if, in fact, they ever were. They were created to meet a popular demand for fecundity, which, put simply, is a demand to make it possible for infertile people who want children to have them. The time has now come to reverse our direction and to stress the perfection and full utilization of antigenerative technologies. This makes the answer to Question 2 an obvious no.

It could be a travesty that at the end of the twentieth century, while reviewing the remarkable advances of medical sciences and arts, all of which have great potential for increasing population, we have simultaneously arrived at the point of overpopulation. The health professions have contributed to the increase in life flow. Now we must call upon them to lend a hand in keeping that flow under control.

18

Matters of Life and Death

In a word, death is one of the most deeply disturbing facts of life. We stand helpless before its irrepressible inevitability. Life-and-death matters are among the principal concerns of every culture. Murder, one form of killing, is motivated to a great extent by impulse, profit, revenge, or pleasure. It has been considered criminal and immoral since the beginnings of history. Manslaughter also is a form of killing that is considered unlawful but committed without malice or forethought. Killing is the annihilation of life. It is permanent and nonrecompensible. If a society fails to deal with murder, including repressing and controlling it, the society could, in time, cease to exist. When is killing not a crime?

We just finished discussing abortion, which is an example of killing. We found it moral and, at the time of this writing, not a crime in our society. Laws of the state require us to kill in time of war. According to ecologically based moral theory, killing in defense of one's country is moral. This is an example of killing as a means of defense and is closely linked to biological necessity and advantage.

Let us now analyze the moral ecology of killing and murder. It will not be necessary to describe or discuss all the methods used in taking life, such as poisoning, hanging, electrocuting, beheading, drowning, and so on. I shall emphasize the differences between legal killing, moral killing, and immoral killing or murder as it is called in criminal law. Using the facts of life and death, I shall demonstrate how a moral principle comes to light in the science of moral ecology. This demonstration will serve as a pattern or general model that can be used in solving moral problems and moral dilemmas.

Let us assume that we are in an actual life-threatening environment and that our perception of its danger is accurate. The moment we become aware of a life-threatening agent in the outer environment, we tend to shift quickly into a defensive behavioral mode. What we decide to do in such a predicament is brought on by the necessity or absolute need to take some kind of defensive action. This is the crucial moment when outer environment stimulates a biological survival or self-preservation reaction. In a situation such as I have described, whatever the characteristics of that reaction, it is moral by definition. Even if we were to run for our lives, plead for leniency, or scream for help, our behavior could certainly not be regarded as immoral. In fact, these reactions might be interpreted as sensible defenses. If our acts were interpreted as cowardly, it would not affect our moral score. In a military battle, however, inappropriate reactions to a life-threatening agent could be regarded as inimical to the purposes and safety of a group and therefore as cowardly and immoral. We are reminded once again that the making of a moral judgment must consider the ecological system in which the event we are judging occurs.

Continuing the analysis of the moral ecology of self-preservation, we shall consider a few of the moral ramifications of loss of life. For example, killing in self-defense has traditionally been regarded as moral. If killing is necessary to survival, it is moral. If it is necessary in the defense of another person or persons, it is also moral. If done by a soldier in the defense of his or her country, it would still be moral. These are classical examples of moral killing that have been factors in human ecology for thousands of years. However, the more recent emergence of huge arsenals of nuclear weapons capable of mass destruction has permanently altered human ecology. We can no longer rationalize every form of killing in national defense. The nuclear age has and will continue to modify our perception of morality.

Understood as the total annihilation of another human being, killing is an extremely serious matter. A civilized person would not kill, even in self-defense, unless there were no available, effective alternative. Killing without the provocation of self-defense or the defense of others, is murder. Murder is generally regarded as the ultimate extremity of injustice and immorality. It eliminates all possibilities of the restitution of the victim's losses.

Note that murder is not a derivative of biological necessity, whereas killing in self-defense is. Murder is a representative example of immorality in general, which is marked by the fact that no immoral act is determined by biological necessity. Arson, kidnapping, rape, fraud, coercion, and all other forms of immoral behavior are not direct reactions to environmental threats, but, instead, are environmental threats themselves. Victims, in turn, must translate such threats into some sort of defense or remedy, which we identify as moral.

This, then, is one of the many distinctions between moral and immoral behavior: *moral behavior is a necessary and beneficial biological (or behavioral) reaction to an environmental threat; immoral behavior is itself a variety of environmental threat.*

The foregoing distinction between morality and immorality is a finding of moral ecology. This finding can be applied in moral decision making. Some examples can be drawn from life and death problems.

The taking of life is of paramount concern historically and in daily affairs. Fear of being murdered or accidentally killed is omnipresent. The search for murderers is a priority of law enforcement. "Thou shall not kill" is a high-ranking sin in all religions. Dealing with the morality of killing and murder, should be simple. It was in earlier times, but not today.

The many facets to acts of self-preservation appear at first to be unsolvable moral dilemmas. For example, is it moral for a starving person to steal food or money with which to buy food? The famous Donner party of American pioneers, marooned by snow in California's high Sierras for the entire winter of 1846 without adequate food supplies, finally resorted to cannibalism. Is this moral?

How does an ecological system of morality analyze these cases? If it is necessary for starving persons to steal food or the money with which to buy it, the act is moral even though usually illegal. In such a case it is probably that the state is immoral, not its starving citizens. Cannibalism, while revolting, is necessary to survival as in the illustration given above, and is therefore moral in those circumstances.

Consider the unlikely case of a starving explorer in the wilds coming upon a hunter who possesses a supply of food. In all probability, the hunter would gladly feed the unfortunate explorer. Suppose, however, that the hunter feels he would jeopardize his own life by depleting his food supply and so refuses to feed the starving man. The latter is now confronted with two environmental threats: starvation and the denial of essential aid. His reaction is to rob the hunter of some food at gunpoint. Would this be a crime or desperate self-defense? The explorer faces a clear-cut example of a double threat to his survival. According to ecological moral theory, the explorer's action is moral. Had he taken all of the food, that would have been immoral; it would have been equivalent to murder. If my scenario had called for the hunter to have willingly shared his food with the explorer, a happy ending would have evolved. Or, the story could have ended in a power struggle between the two men in which one or the other or both died.

The clashing of humans can become chaotic and produce a rather hapless, amoral predicament where the borders of rationality and irrationality are blurred. If either the hunter or the explorer had emerged from such a conflict alive, could we say, to the victor has gone the spoils, but not necessarily the accolade "moral"? Would that be given to the explorer had he emerged alive? Both men would have shifted between the roles of "moral subject" and "threatening agent" a number of times thus blurring a final judgment. This happens on the battlefield where, finally, the brave are cited, not the moral or immoral. On a battlefield both sides presumably regard themselves as moral, though the preoccupation of soldiers is killing or being killed. The immorality of war is not to be found so much on the battlefield as in the seats of political power.

Some situations defy simple moral analysis. Suicide or self-killing is a case in point. Suicide is always a possibility when a person sees few advantages to life in comparison to the disadvantages, when the pain of existence outweighs the pleasures, or when rewards are few and penalties are overwhelming. Whatever the reasons—they are too many to discuss here—suicide in and of itself is moral. Those who fail at attempting suicide may be making a desperate bid for attention and help. The right to commit suicide is not permitted under law, but successful suicide is naturally beyond the reach of law. The right to suicide is self-conferred. Anyone who decides on suicide can follow through without anyone granting permission.

Regardless of the cause, when people die they may leave behind individuals who are adversely affected by the death. We do not declare a dead person immoral for having died and for having left suffering behind. When suicides leave suffering people behind them, their acts of suicide are commonly regarded as immoral. Should we think, feel, and act differently following death by suicide and death in general? A rational, moral ecology answer to this question is both yes and no; yes if suicides, in taking their lives, cause dependents and others great harm; no if they do not have dependents and close family ties. No fine line between the two can be drawn. Suicide is commonly regarded as tragic. We stretch the imagination to see it as criminal, and it is not always immoral. (Matters brought up in this paragraph might be worth discussing in suicide prevention counseling.)

No party, including the state, is justified in attempting to prevent suicide. Coercive suicide prevention is immoral because it interferes needlessly with the rights of suicides to control and manage their own lives. However, nothing is immoral about suicide counseling if the relationship of counselor and subject is voluntary.*

A Pennsylvania official under legal investigation shot himself to death at a press conference in 1987. This suicide was shown on television and photographs of the event were published in newspapers, starting a debate about the appropriateness of the media coverage of this event. Was it moral to make a public show of this personal tragedy? Certainly no harm could be done to the dead man. It would be difficult to prove that serious harm was done to anyone. The reporters' rush to tell and show was not considerate of the feelings of the victim's family and could be judged in poor taste. Perhaps this man wanted to shock accusers, those at the press conference, and those in the media audience. This seems a likely conclusion. If anyone could be judged "immoral," it would be the suicide: not for taking his own life, but for the public display of violence which could distress viewers.

It is not unusual to hear people express a death wish. I have heard many people of various ages, even young children, say, "I wish I were dead." Such exclamations are most likely when the subjects are frustrated, angry, disappointed, and seriously disabled, or feel rejected, undesirable, or socially defeated.

Ahead of actual self-killing in sheer numbers are those individuals of all ages who turn their frustrations and hostility against themselves through self-neglect, withdrawal from social life, alcohol and drug addiction, dropping out from educational and career pursuits, and the like. This is a form of silent suicide and, in many, a prelude to self-killing.

In the United States, the rate of suicide is highest in people over age sixty-five. Elderly persons are frequently overwhelmed with depressing circumstances; poverty; the loss of loved ones and friends; the depreciation of intellectual, physical, and sensory acuity; and painful and irreversible diseases. The mental health of older people in our society is neglected. Many elderly fail to take medications, to follow their physician's advice, to eat nutritious meals, and to exercise enough. Such behavior is in the realm of silent suicide.

Many terminally ill patients of all age groups want to die and they

---

*See Thomas Szasz, "The Case Against Suicide Prevention," *American Psychologist* (July 1986).

occasionally succeed in killing themselves. The elderly are probably more highly motivated and determined to end it all, which may account for their greater success record. Suicides among the elderly are a way to break out of the prison of life. Those who take this matter into their own hands cannot be accused of immorality.

This brings us to euthanasia, which is the science and art of assisting a person to die who wants to die. In our society this is just another example of complicating a simple moral principle. In the Judeo-Christian tradition, God gives life and only God should take it away. The trouble is, God does not make it easy to bear the suffering of certain terminal disorders including just plain everyday old age. If a person earnestly expresses a desire to die, he or she should be allowed to do so. It is moral to exercise the right to terminate your life and it is the one right you can confer upon yourself. Life during the final months and days of a terminal illness is an abomination. It is immoral to force a dying person to drag it out. The fear that euthanasia will be abused is unfounded. We have in our country thousands of capable physicians, public health experts, lawyers, religionists, and bioethicists who could easily work out a socially responsible, fail-safe system of beneficent euthanasia. An alternative to euthanasia is the hospice, where pain is controlled by a medically supervised program and the patient is allowed to die naturally.

In a sane society, the constitutional right to life should be accompanied by the corresponding right to die. When people are reaching the end of their days and are psychologically ready to die, they should be granted the legal right to die without a tangle of legal red tape and other noxious burdens. Mercy killing should be included in any rational, fail-safe program of euthanasia. This would eliminate the crime of a well spouse killing a sick spouse who begs and cries for death.

Another moral problem related to euthanasia is the death sentence for certain criminals. As a typical example, let us keep in mind the serial killer. The term *death sentence* is a frank admission that we want to eliminate the horrible troublemaker; besides, it is more realistic than the term *capital punishment*. It is not clear how a dead man is supposed to find out that he has been punished, or if punishment merely refers to a form of legal/social revenge against the criminal. Numerous citizens have to be separated from society at large. If people have, in all ordinary ways, proved themselves incapable of civilized behavior, they must be separated from their fellow humans for life, or by death if they request it.

If a life termer should request death in preference to life imprisonment, the question arises, by whose hand? Such a preference is logical and moral. The prisoner is not coerced with respect to his decision. Who would care to argue which of the two alternatives, life imprisonment or death, is superior? And should society choose one over the other? Let us assume the prisoner decides to die. No painless method of assisting a criminal to die would be immoral. Such an assisted suicide could be conducted by prison personnel, with or without witnesses, or the presence of members of the prisoner's family and friends. If life termers choose death, they should share in deciding the method of assisted suicide and in deciding who will be invited to be present at their death.

Should a person kill another in revenge? A man attempted to kill the killer of his daughter. The father did not do this in self-defense or in defense of his daughter. According to the principles of moral ecology, the father's act was immoral, though understandable.

Immolation and public suicide have been practiced for centuries as a means of attracting attention to religious and political causes and to perhaps encourage the support of witnesses. The exigencies of warfare call for horrendous sacrifices on a massive scale. During the early days of the war in South Vietnam, Buddhist priests practiced immolation in public as a political protest. They exercised a self-conferred right to burn themselves to death as a dramatic political protest. Sacrificing the self for a cause in which one believes has generally been regarded as moral and heroic. Christ did it: Christian evangelists like to say that Christ gave his life for us. In an ecological moral system self-sacrifice is moral, though history may raise questions concerning the importance of the results of such sacrifices.

It would be remiss to close this chapter on life and death without commenting briefly on the secondary victims of murder and other criminal acts. So often in the commission of immoral acts, it is not just the immediate victim who is injured, but witnesses, close relatives, and associates who are secondary victims of the act. In making a moral assessment of behavioral interactions, we must look beneath the surface of primary victims to the harm or injury sustained by certain secondary victims. I am especially concerned with adverse psychological reactions to shock. Emotional shock can be dangerous. It could trigger a heart attack or upset an individual's neuroendocrinal balance, which could lead to painful, long-term emotional stress, psychosomatic illness, reduced job efficiency, and so on.

The harm and loss of both primary and secondary victims of crime are a major concern of the law, and they play a prominent role in judging and sentencing criminals. It has been and still is a common practice to use incidences of secondary harm in further condemnation of immoral behavior. However, in the last quarter of this century, secondary harm has become a popular accusation among plaintiffs in law suits in which restitution for every conceivable loss and injury is demanded.

Such cases bring up intriguing and difficult questions for law, government, and politics, but not difficult or unusual problems for moral ecology. In moral ecology theory the primary function of the state is the protection of the lives and property of its citizens. When this function fails, the state is obligated morally to help its stricken citizens. The baseline of moral ecology as a science is to isolate and describe the criteria of moral and immoral behavior. Exploitative and self-seeking demands for restitution from crime victims is immoral. It is not the function of government to enrich or glorify crime victims, but to offer them palliative assistance to a self-sufficient adjustment to life, if possible.

In examining the aftermath of any crime, we must realize that the restoration of all conditions to the way they were before the crime is impossible. Any of us can be victims of accidents and criminal activity. We cannot reasonably expect to be insured against all the vicissitudes of chance and against all our own follies and misjudgments.

Legal problems created by liability suits resemble those created in the field of defense law. Every imaginable strategy has been used by defense attorneys to reduce the severity of sentences of convicted murderers and other criminals. The object of such strategies has been to prove that defendants are not wholly responsible for committing their crimes and, therefore, are deserving of lighter sentences. Among the common excuses used in reducing the penalties of murderers, for instance, are insanity, diminished capacity, neurohormonal imbalances (example: hypoglycemia), substance abuse, jealousy, and humiliation. These excuses also are termed extenuating circumstances and contingent or contributing factors. Defense maneuvers, no matter how resourceful and emotionally compelling, cannot diminish the immorality of murder and other serious crimes. (Problems arising from the rapidly expanding subjugation and exploitation of law by the legal professions are taken up again in Part Four, "Conquering Moral Problems.")

Looking back over the last two chapters, we recognize anew that moral principles involve behaviors and interpersonal relationships that trigger strong emotions and prejudices of all kinds. Moral ecology, however, takes no notice of what are commonly called affairs of the heart. Any act taken at random is either moral or immoral. We must first judge the morality of an act by ecologically based moral law. When we doubt the dicta of moral law, or feel that this law should be toned down, we then question our personal sensitivity to the emotions and prejudices that have arisen.

The various ways we respond to human interactions obscure our understanding of the moral factors involved. When emotions and prejudices rule, rational, moral analysis of a situation is stalled or terminated. In approaching the analysis of any moral problem it is wise for us to first objectively apply ecologically derived moral principles. If the resultant findings seem too harsh, we next re-examine the origins, functions, and purposes of our sensitivity. This process brings to mind the difficulties of escaping from old, habitual ways of believing, thinking, and feeling.

19

Property, Profit, and Morals

Why include a chapter on property and profit in a book on morals? Some of the best thinkers of the twentieth century have a constricted view of property. They see property as inanimate or nonhuman, while the animate —the human body and mind—is viewed as something unconnected with and apart from material things. Likewise, the meaning of profit is unduly narrowed to some kind of economic gain or advantage, which is often looked down on as, at best, a necessary evil. This chapter is designed, in part, to rectify these extremely limited views of property and profit.

The answer to the above question, however, is that property and profit pervade every aspect of human behavior and moral thought. Property is what morality and law are all about. Whenever we talk about morals, we will inevitably raise the subject of property. And profit is what life is all about; without it we would languish and die. A life devoid of pleasure, gratification, love, gain, advantage, success, satisfaction—in a word, profit —would be formidably bleak and painful. I am therefore widening the meanings of property and profit. This will be increasingly the case as we move on.

Property is not just physical objects, such as land, buildings, jewelry, stock certificates, and bank accounts, but the ownership of such objects by individuals or by a group of people. The ownership (the having, the holding, the possessing) of things is what establishes them as property. Either we own ourselves or are slaves to others. The mere fact that we own or belong to ourselves makes us a kind of private property. Life itself is what makes possible the ownership of anything. At this point, we can observe that there is no such entity as unowned property, or ownership without life.

The ownership of the self is determined by many factors, such as nature's gift of life and the moral quality of the human ecosystem into which we are born. If we succeed in surviving, we may come into possession of many things by creating them ourselves and by acquiring them from others. The security of our property, like life itself, is ultimately dependent on our ability to defend it, which, in turn, is largely dependent on favorable environmental support.

The integrity of all organisms depends on a supportive environment that favors life rather than death. Another biological fact is our ownership of ourselves. A derivative of this latter fact, and of equal importance to it, is that every thing that emanates from our creative powers, with the exception of our offspring, belongs to us and is our personal property to keep, give away, sell, abandon, or destroy. This concept of property is also a fact of human ecology. It is basic to a proper understanding of government, law, and the ecology of morals.

Land is a gift of nature, as is life. All other forms of property were created by humans as necessities, advantages, and life enhancers. Our institution of law allows us to own land under certain circumstances and to sell it, give it away, or abandon it. Obviously, the ownership of land, as well as everything else, ends with the owner's death. Land then goes to other owners or back to abiotic nature.

The concept of property is not just a convention, as is frequently contended. Property derives from an extension of our organismic reach into the natural environment in a search for security, comfort, and self-expression. Property is not a mere convention, but life itself plus possessions that make living not only bearable but worthwhile. Humans produce all property except land and its attendant natural resources. In a strict sense, property comes into existence only as the result of human creativity and effort.

Law is an institution created and nurtured by government for the sole purpose of protecting citizens' rights to have and hold property. No government succeeds completely in protecting the lives and other property rights of its citizens. Even in the modern world only a small percentage of citizens have the capability of protecting what they own. Probably government was always fostered and tolerated for the purpose of protecting property. This is the perennial human ecology theme of government. It seems to prevail despite the historic frequency of the perversion of government as a power base for special privilege. Using an expanded definition of property to include the human organism and all other forms of property, we can conclude that the whole institution of law is concerned with protecting property rights, nothing else.

The concept that people are a form of property is as old as slavery. The related idea that the ownership of self is a prerogative to be fought for is embodied in the abolition of slavery. While the concept of self-ownership is not yet generally realized, it is essential to an ecological system of morals, which holds that our ownership of self, all that we create with our minds and bodies, and all material things we come to possess by moral means, should be ours to rule over and control. To some degree this is true in today's world. We can give or sell our products, goods, services, and other possessions and enter into agreements and contracts with regard to such transactions. We are free, with minimal limits, to enter or exit various kinds of interpersonal relationships. Thus, a wide choice of goods and services is open to us, yet all around us there are numerous roadblocks to freedom.

Our inner environment of emotions, sensations, perceptions, beliefs, memories, opinions, thoughts, conceptions, and ideas are personal property. These are personal possessions; our minds are loaded with such property. We can consciously choose to conceal this inner world or divulge all of it if we wish. Ideas are part of our inner world. They are special products of thinking and include concepts, problem solutions, theories, and hypotheses. Ideas as property are important concerns of law and morality.

It is difficult to prove or defend claims to the originality and uniqueness of ideas. Another difficulty: once someone else's idea has been revealed to us and we approve of it and perceive its importance, it becomes a part of us. We find it extremely difficult, if not impossible, to detach our thinking and acting from the influence of ideas once they are thoroughly accepted as truth. Even if we disagree with someone's bright idea, it might remain in memory as a part of our store of knowledge. We are all engaged in learning from others throughout life. This is a part of what we mean by the phrase, "learning from experience." The day comes when it is impossible to trace all our thoughts and ideas back to their sources. To attempt to do so would leave little time for anything else. Our indebtedness to others who have advanced our skills and knowledge can frequently be identified, and when this can be done it is moral to credit the source. It is immoral to palm off as our own the ideas of others.

Is it possible to protect one's ideas? Yes, but no more so than any other form of property. A safe deposit box might protect our documents and jewelry. The equivalent protection for an idea would be to keep it secret. History shows that every valuable idea, once revealed, ultimately finds its way into the common currency of human thought. An idea cannot be copyrighted or patented. It must first be transformed into a palpable product, such as an invention, a manufacturing process, or works of art, literature, and science that are recorded in print or by any other means of media technology before it can qualify for protection under patent or copyright law.

There is literally no end to the process of widening our perspective of property and profit. There is hardly anything that escapes becoming property or profit to someone. Going back to the beginnings of the written word, we will find references to property and belongings. Slavery indicates that people were regarded as property. People speak of themselves as giving their lives to a cause or of losing their lives. Phrases like "my head," "my arms," "my life" indicate that there is some conscious awareness among people of belonging to themselves. It is likely that ancient people thought of themselves as property. Under ancient Babylonian laws, for example, individuals could sell themselves into slavery and also buy their way out of it.

An ancient urban freeman citizen was a consumer, producer, user, trader, and hoarder of property. He could own several wives, concubines, and many children. He could buy or sell slaves and any of his real or personal property, including wives and children. In some ancient legal systems, the main wife and her children could inherit the master's property. Under the laws of Hammurabi, inheritance was handled "justly" by courts of law. Each free, propertied person was expected to treat those in his household or estate like a good father would treat a family. This kind of behavior is an approach to a moral principle recognizing that we can be little or nothing without earning the support of others; that even though we control others we cannot neglect their care without risking the disintegration of basic social structures.

In ancient urban civilizations people worked and schemed to profit from life, to support families, to acquire useful objects, fulfillment of desires, money, skills, learning, friends, and leadership standing. Many individuals accumulated considerable wealth and power. Property and the desire to possess and use it invited every conceivable means of acquiring it other than through moral and legal means. War, plunder, piracy, coercion, robbery, extortion, and fraud were popular means of acquiring the property of others. They were short-cuts to profit, and are still universally practiced.

The rise of high-density urban populations was accompanied by an increase of all kinds of property and means of gaining profits. Property and profits were erroneously blamed for immoral behavior and often fell heir to a bad reputation, which survives to this day. Readers familiar with the economics of Christ's time will recall the usurious interest rates of the money lenders and the predatory practices of the tax collectors. In those times it was as hard to keep property as it was to get hold of it in the first place. One consequence of this predicament, as time went on, was the willingness of property owners to vest government with sufficient power to protect property and to put up with the tax burdens of supporting state protection.

A governmental goal of every genuine civilization in history was to provide effective means of protecting all forms of property. Any failure of government to achieve its end resulted in chaos and barbarism. Without the protection of all forms of property, including, of course, one's body, life would have little if any value. Government comes close to a bioenvironmental definition of a moral element. Perhaps it is one of the most important of all moral discoveries. If anything exists because of necessity, it is government. But it does not need to be a form of government that is practiced today.

Beginning with the Renaissance, the Age of Exploration, and, later, the Industrial Revolution, the definition of property and the laws and means of protecting it began to take on many modern-day characteristics. In Western Europe, including England, it was not until the eighteenth century that the strict modern laws of ownership, property transfer, inheritance, and protection of property took on forms very much like those we use today.

The development of commerce and urban societies took place side by side. It was a slow, complex process that included the emergence of specialized crafts and skills in food production, housing, manufacturing, transport, business, trade, the arts, education, and more. All of these commercial activities became interdependent. Collectively, they provided additional avenues for human environmental outreach and exploration, and, in time, additional sources of human necessities, advantages, and life enhancements. All of these developments contributed to the expansion and versatility of the human ecosystem. Much of what we call civilization could not have existed without commerce: the production, buying, selling, and transporting of goods and the concomitant employment and use of human services.

Business people expect to profit from their work. There are no benevolent businesses. If a business is unprofitable, it is failing and will soon be bankrupt. In a free enterprise system, profits are determined by market conditions. If a business develops an especially profitable market for its goods and services, others will quickly compete for a share of the market and their action may moderate prices, but not, necessarily, deplete profits.

Profit is the principal motive behind all human activity. The word *all* may seem a little far-fetched, but let me explain. A profit results from acquiring something we want, or from doing something we want to do. Profit adds enjoyment to life and it can be enjoyment itself. It is doubtful that anyone does anything for no profit whatsoever. No act is selfless. Even giving is a form of pleasure, or, perhaps, a beneficial corrective for a guilty conscience. In doing something for a loved one, the profit is the joy of expressing love for the other person. Sister Theresa won a Nobel Prize (1985) for giving her life to aiding the weak and unfortunate. She must feel that her religiously inspired humanitarian service is intensely rewarding. The English philosopher Thomas Hobbes (1588–1679) believed that no human being gives but with the intention of benefiting himself. Much later the Dutch philosopher Benedict Spinoza (1632–1677) declared that human beings do everything toward the end that is profitable. Similar ideas were expounded in Roman times.

In everyday life, profits are usually thought of as gains from business transactions. In the foregoing text the word *profit* has been considerably expanded beyond its common meaning in economics. As I have noted before, profit is essential to life. It is a crown jewel of morality held in its natural setting in biological necessity. There is no way to profit from any undertaking without affecting someone's property, or, possibly, our own. Since all property belongs to someone, to even qualify as property, we cannot affect the property of others without affecting them. Adversely affecting the property of others is equivalent to affecting them adversely in a personal sense. Primordial property and all other forms of property are bound together. The harmful results of transgressions against property cannot be confined to a targeted property. All invasions of others' property rights are immoral without the owners' knowledge and consent, even though the outcomes are benign.

Fortunately, buying and selling property can work to the advantage of all parties concerned. This had better be true since producing goods and providing services for consumers is a principal activity of humankind. Buying and selling goods and services are what economics is all about, from the corner grocery to the World Bank. The motivation for all this activity is profit: wages, salary, interest, dividends, or what is left in a business account after all expenses and taxes have been paid. It is indeed beautiful when economic activities redound to the benefit of all. If this sort of condition were universal, we would be on the way to achieving a moral world.

An example of a moral business deal shall not be amiss here. It can stand as a benchmark for morality in business. I have chosen the rather simple business of selling a house. A number of specialty services can be involved in such a transaction: a real estate broker, a title insurance company, an escrow officer, perhaps a mortgage and loan company, an attorney, an advertising medium, and, of course, a seller and a buyer. A couple who no longer need a large home decide to sell it through a real estate broker. The latter locates a buyer. A mutually acceptable sales price and other arrangements are made. In the end, all parties to the deal are satisfied, all were free to enter or not enter the various agreements and no one feels unrewarded.

Occasionally we will read that a well-known, large corporation is making obscenely high profits. There is a tendency in business to "charge all that the traffic will bear." For instance, hotel and motel rates vary with the time of year, rising during the tourist season. In 1973, we could read in the press how staid old American oil companies "gouged" and "profiteered" during the Middle East oil embargoes. There is an ongoing scourge of obscene profits from criminal operations such as drug trafficking, illicit gambling, assorted con games, insider stock market trading, and the like. These activities are obviously immoral, flagrantly hurting large numbers of victims. But there are numerous so-called legitimate business operations that make huge profits that are morally questionable even though legal. A few of these are arbitrage; hostile corporation takeovers; entrepreneurial schemes that make money through tax evasion, fraud, and dependence on inflationary trends. These operations have common components that are, essentially, making profits from the losses of others and acquiring wealth without the production of goods and services that benefit society. Further, business schemes, the success of which rely on inflationary trends, tend to abet inflation, thus increasing the potency of that malicious by-product of governmental fiscal irresponsibility.

Downright plunder and legitimate, customary business profits often get blurred in the minds of social critics who become impatient with the slow correctives of a free enterprise system, such as competition. Karl Marx and his mid-nineteenth-century treatise *Das Kapital* gave property and profits the low ratings they had come to deserve. The horrendous exploitation of labor by early industrial capitalists, which spurred Marx's attacks, simmered down after the rise of powerful labor unions. In the twentieth century, labor unions became so powerful they could paralyze large segments of the economy if their demands were not met by employers. Many other changes took place. Business management became more humane. It also developed mass production, lower product costs, and ingenious marketing techniques that lead to greater earnings for workers and greater benefits to consumers.

The economic ills of society cannot be blamed on property and profit anymore than substance abuse can be blamed on drugs, or sex crimes on sexuality, or obesity on food. Such societal ills as avarice, crime, lust for power, and poverty must be charged to immorality, which extends from the seats of government to our city slums. It is the operations performed in transferring property and acquiring profit that are moral or immoral. If we were to regard profit-making as immoral, then most everything we do for almost every reason would be immoral by definition.

It is commonly believed that one person's loss is another's gain and vice versa. Gains and losses are experiences of every living thing. There is no way to eliminate our vulnerability to loss: the loss of our lives, the lives of loved ones, and our loss of material property. We are vulnerable to many types of ecological change: peace and war, health and illness, or what insurance companies call acts of God. Chance plays an important role in accidents, employment, and the success of investments. It is not rational to believe that all our losses and misfortunes represent gains for others, or that all our gains come at the expense of others. If we could not accept loss as a natural phenomenon we would not be able to endure life.

I question the myths of nonprofit and not-for-profit organizations. Administrators and salaried employees of large nonprofit foundations, trusts, privately endowed institutions, and religious establishments are certainly not donating their time and talent to the cause. Many such nonprofit enterprises are weighted with freeloaders and self-aggrandizing management cliques who seem in some instances to dupe patrons into providing seed money for new expansion ventures. Up front these organizations look as good as those of the for-profit species. Not-for-profit work forces are frequently supplemented by volunteer workers. A main administrative nonprofit goal is to avoid showing a monetary profit and thus escape taxation. Their real profit is counted in the value of their services and products to society. Millions of volunteer workers also enjoy profits in the satisfaction of interesting and socially useful work. Paradoxically, non-profit enterprise is hallowed in our society. It is regarded as elevated, in a moral sense, above enterprise for profit. This is no doubt due, in part, to the negative constructions we have learned to place on the meaning of the word *profit*. If taxation were eliminated, the differences between profit and nonprofit organizations would hardly be distinguishable. All establishments exist for profit. They just have different methods and standards of measuring it.

This chapter has been devoted to explaining the nature of property and profit, their relationship to human behavior, and, particularly, to morality. Up to this point, I have shown that all forms of crime—in fact, all forms of immorality—involve property of some kind in some way, and that people engage in crime for the sake of profit. From these facts we may deduce that efforts to reduce crime must include means for taking the profit out of crime. A starting point is the optimal protection of all forms of property.

Not unlike past centuries, we live in an age of physical danger and insufficient regard for the property of others. This extends from the lofty halls of Congress, where our representatives refuse to obey their own laws, to humble corridors lined with high school lockers. Just how can we go about improving the protection of primordial and material property? First, by continuing to improve all aspects of law, jurisprudence, and law enforcement. Second, by improving moral education. Beyond these means, we can count on a proliferation of scientific crime detection and prevention technology, such as home and business protection systems that not only detect intruders and warn security forces of a break-in, but actually incapacitate burglars, thus automatically isolating them with hidden mechanical barriers. We can also expect more improvements in electronic surveillance devices.

The big question is: Will we have the courage to take the profit out of every type of crime? Would we sanction a radical strategy to stop drug trafficking: for example, by establishing an aggressively competitive, publicly supported drug market? Or, would we abolish tax supported aid to those who choose to handicap or destroy themselves through substance abuse; self-determined risks to life and limb; and through property losses attributable to ignorance and poor judgment?

These stringent and unappealing proposals to reduce the profit in crime are at odds with our permissive lifestyle. Nevertheless, we may soon be forced to decide whether we want a crime-ridden community or a sane society. When the time comes we shall be justified, morally, in employing any means necessary to create a safe and peaceful society.

Recall once more the basic morality of property and profit. They are at the center of human biological necessities and organismic fulfillment. They stretch across the whole continuum of morality. That they were ever regarded as the cause of immorality is one of the most troublesome hand-me-downs of history. Property is not only something that is owned, it is used to make life more profitable. A thing cannot be called property unless it is owned and therein lies the moral connection. Morality concerns how property is transferred from one owner to another. Any transfer effected by force, coercion, fraud, or similar strategy is immoral because it violates the property prerogatives of others.

To reach out and acquire the necessities and pleasures of life is as much dictated by our biological structure as by our social structures (institutions). We are acquisitive like all other organisms. Acquisitiveness is a powerful part of human nature. However, acquisitive behaviors that threaten the security and well-being of others are all examples of immoral behavior. There are no exceptions. This fact requires that all forms of immoral behavior be viewed as inimical to civilization and that strong effective measures to subdue and ultimately eradicate it must be persistently carried forward. The will and power to do this are basic to the preservation and improvement of civilization.

One way to further moral education is to legitimize the profit motive, to elevate it to the status of a moral element, which, in truth, it is. The nucleus of moral behavior is enlightened self-interest, which means to be for the self, to nurture and empower the self in every moral way. These injunctions do not infer that being for the self necessitates in any way being against others. In fact, the surest way to defeat the self, in the long run, is to be against others, to win out at their expense. The profit motive is a powerful tool to use, not only in teaching moral behavior but in psychotherapy.

The psychologist A. Bandura has presented convincing evidence that people can be changed by goal seeking and by striving for highly prized benefits.* Feelings of inferiority and lack of confidence are usually accompanied by anxiety and fear. These emotions, with all their complicated physiological and mental correlates, can be moderated by ideas and social

---

American Psychologist (December 1986).

persuasion that raise levels of beneficial expectation. The motivation to gain or profit from a course of action may reduce fear.

Damage to or loss of property is felt by the owner as personal injury. Thieves, vandals, arsonists, and the like prey on material property, not directly on people. Even pickpockets avoid contact with their victims if possible. This is a class of crime in which the criminal does not plan to harm victims physically, though such criminals may resort to physical violence if caught committing a crime. This category of crime fits the ecological format of immorality: the agent is not impelled to act out of biological necessity and the victim sustains both primordial and material property loss. Victims can suffer from both economic loss and negative psychosomatic and physical reactions.

No form of human motivation is immoral unless its expression harms or injures others; no form of privately, jointly, or publicly owned property is immoral unless creating, controlling, or using it harms or injures others. Examples of what I mean by harm or injury include violating the property rights of others and curtailing their liberty.

If we profit from the property losses of others, we have committed a crime; if anyone makes a profit at our expense by directly causing us to lose property, we are victims of crime.* We are all potential victims of immoral and illegal behavior, such as breaking agreements and contracts, slander, threats, coercion, fraud, and treachery. Any kind of a market can be corrupted by shoddy merchandise, dishonest advertising, and misleading guarantees. The insider traders in the stock market can rob us of the opportunity to fully profit from corporation stock we may own. Some entrepreneurial real estate partnerships make millions of dollars for their principal operators without these people producing any goods or services other than the profits extracted from the economic damage of victims such as real estate renters and corporation employees. In some cases such profits may be immoral even though legal.

No matter how much the profit motive may benefit an individual, it does not guarantee that the results will be moral. After all, crime in every form is motivated by the desire for profit. What profit the criminal obtains is at the cost of the property of others, which again clearly indicates that the way to stop crime is to take the profit out of it. The im-

---

*Gambling is an exception to this observation. Gambling is a special case since the laws of chance rule profit and loss, not the intent to harm self or others, though these factors are an ever-present risk to gamblers.

morality of crime is not caused by property but by trampling over the property rights of others.

Criminality may be looked upon as one of many alternate ways of making a living in our society. According to a Justice Department report released in April of 1987, 1.2 million robberies occurred annually in the United States from 1973 to 1984. That is a lot of crime but it's nothing compared to the sum total of crime committed in the country at large. There is no profession or occupation, from the world of banking and high finance to science and religion, that does not have its share of bona fide criminals.

In summary, we create property to gain the necessities of life, to gain advantages, or to enhance the quality of life. We may look upon the property we acquire as advancing the art of living, which, if finally learned, is the ultimate profit. No rational person strives for nonprofit and a disordered life. Property is not just a social convention, but an integral part of the bio-environmental continuum.

It is now possible to see that today's morality maze exists largely because we do not equate property with the life sciences. Property is usually treated as part of the subject matter of the social sciences, behavioral sciences, economics, law and religion, and as, more or less, a convention or custom devoid of biological connections. The separation of primordial property and material property—the animate versus the inanimate form of property mentioned in the beginning of this chapter—is illogical since one cannot exist without the other. This confusion has retarded the social and life sciences. The persistence of this course will continue to weaken the success and credibility of the social sciences. Some ramifications of this trend were discussed in chapter 16. A fact worth repeating here is that the fine line separating human life from human environment is rapidly disappearing.

The total concept of property and profit is rooted in human ecology. If we stretch our imaginations, we can say that what we call the social sciences are also rooted in human ecology. This means that the scientific base of morality, property, and the social sciences is biology. It would be impossible to have a science of humankind that ignored primordial property and its organismic connections to all other kinds of property. Also, it is biologically impossible for human life to exist without property, profit, and morality. We can speak of this concept as the principle of the "contiguity of property."

20

The Ecology of Morals

The reactions of human beings to their total environment of self, others, and the surrounding natural world constitute the phenomenal territory of human ecology. The interdependency of self, others, and the biotic and abiotic phenomena of our natural habitat are the sources of our psychological and social life, and, consequently, our moral behavior. The study of morals in the setting of human ecology places morality in the natural sciences rather than in philosophy. In human ecology, moral principles emerge as a body of natural law. Human ecology, the science of the interactions and interdependence of the human organism and its total environment, is the scientific base of moral ecology.

Our biological nature leaves us no alternative but to follow its laws if we wish to survive. We must have air, water, nutrition, rest, shelter, minimal safety, health, strength, and the means of obtaining these things. We also possess strong tendencies and desires that demand attention and fulfillment, such as a tendency to seek attachments, to gain social control, and to protect our property. There is also the desire for freedom and for sexual expression. Basic provisions for the support of life are not options but absolute necessities. All that we are required to do by our biological nature as an aid to survival is a response to natural law, over which we have no recourse but to obey.

Strictly biological requirements for organismic survival do not markedly change with time. They are constant and absolute. We must meet the demands of nature if we want to live: self-preservation is a moral imperative. Thus, at a very fundamental level, we can see that morality is a function of the interaction of biological laws and complex environmental factors that together undergird the whole structure of human ecology.

The tremendous importance of all forms of property in human ecology is highlighted by the following illustration: if all the people on Earth were eliminated, property would cease to exist. All physical objects created by humans and all human meanings that have been given form would become mere things detached from any human use or significance. There is, indeed, a close relationship between people, material property, and the personal experience of profit and benefit. In fact, property and all else that is identified with human beings cannot be understood except as a function of the interaction of the human organism and its total environment.

I cannot overemphasize that an understanding of moral ecology requires an understanding of property and profit, which are not only features of humankind's total environment but are major factors in the human ecological system. If we understand the nature of our total environment of self, others, and our earthly habitat, and also understand the characteristics of property and profit, we possess the background for an understanding of morality. This can be achieved without reference to moral philosophy or religious doctrines and beliefs.

There is no interaction between humans that does not involve property and profit, nor a form of either that is immune to becoming a factor in moral behavior. This strongly indicates that property, profit, morality, and the human organism are inextricably connected; that morals are the central connective or mediative mechanism of human interactions; and that moral elements mediate all transactions and communications between human beings and their total environment. The latter, of course, encompasses all forms of property, both that belonging to the self and that belonging to others. Thus, morality is a function of humans coping with the totality of their environment.

In chapter 7 the example of a single, isolated human was used to illustrate some basic facts of morality. Such a person—let's call him George—would not have to account to anyone for his behavior. George could commit no murder, take no material property from others, or be a victim of the immorality of others. I then added one other person to the picture, and, finally, others to make up a small primitive tribe. In the social situation comprised of two or more people, mutual benefits arose. One could picture improvements in food supplies, protection techniques, division of responsibilities, and other signs of moral behavior. One could also imagine bickering, fighting, stealing, and murder. It was in the interpersonal relations of group members that moral behavior arose as the means of facilitating the essential operations of daily living, without which the group would languish and eventually perish.

Moral principles and behaviors are derivatives of biological necessity. This, too, was illustrated in chapter 7 with the story of a primitive mother caring for her baby. Nurturing a baby is a series of behavioral operations without which humankind would not have survived. Obviously, such caring is a biological necessity, an imperative in life flow. Other biological necessities were described, such as food production, self-defense, protection of self and others, sexual unions, divisions of labor, and so on. The phrase "the taproot of morality is biological necessity" was used, thereby launching a gradual unfolding of an ecological science of morality.

The concept of self-ownership and of the self as a form of property is essential to an ecological system of morals. Ownership of self extends to all property we personally create with our bodies and minds or property that we acquire from others by moral means. All our personal material property is but the result of our reaching out into the environment in a search for such benefits as security, comfort, and self-expression. Our primordial property would be at risk if we were denied all material property, which would include, of course, all forms of sustenance. This fact urges us to accept as an ecological moral premise the idea that society must protect our natural prerogative to own and control all our property, primordial and material, providing that in so doing, we do not undermine the property holdings of others.

Once we recognize that all property is integral to our total environment, we are in possession of a fundamental fact of our ecosystem. In that system lies all our property and opportunity for profit. When the privilege of controlling our property is threatened by an agent in our outer environment, we are morally justified in countering that threat. This is a basic moral principle. Acting upon it, however, is thwarted by powerful environmental forces, such as criminal activity and government.

Acquisitive behaviors that threaten the security and well-being of others are immoral. There appears to be no exception to this principle. Common examples are fraud, theft, embezzlement, con-games, graft, hostile corporate takeovers, conspiracy, and insider stock market trading. These are treacherous forms of property transfers, but usually they do not involve direct physical harm. There are many forms of acquisitive behavior, however, that employ coercion and physical force: e.g., mugging, hijacking, drug trafficking, kidnapping, rape, murder, and war. The main objective of immoral acquisitive behavior is to obtain the property of others without consent or recompense.

All crime is committed without the consent or compensation of victims. Crime exacts a staggering price upon victims who suffer a loss of property: the profit from the use of property; the time and effort expended in acquiring property; the depreciation of psychological and physical health; and, in some cases, even the loss of their most valuable possession, life itself. It is this cost to victims that focuses attention on the threat that crime is to the efficacy of human ecology. In a biological sense, morality works *for* humankind, immorality *against*.

Property and profit are components of all behavior, moral and immoral, noncriminal and criminal, the chief difference being that the immoral and criminal acquisition of property and profit are achieved at the expense of the property and profit of others. The matter of transferring property from one owner to another is the most significant concern of applied morality. Any transfer of property that is actuated by force, coercion, fraud, or other harmful stratagems is immoral.

In chapter 17 our attention was directed to the flagrant abuse of those features of our natural environment that we are obliged by the nature of things to share with all members of our species: specifically, the atmosphere, the oceans, potable water supplies, energy, and other resources in which we have a fundamental common biological need. The abuses I spoke of are environmental pollution and the overdraft of natural resources, both of which are usually, but not always, the result of overpopulation.

Biologist Garrett Hardin,[*] one of the first scientists to discover ecologically derived moral principles, advanced verifiable evidence to prove that future ecosystem disasters cannot be avoided by new technologies. We must in a thoroughgoing manner rethink the moral imperatives of survival and the means of actualizing them. Ecosystem protection requires public and political acceptance of new moral conceptions that eclipse many moral standards of earlier times.

Unrestrained population growth leads quickly and directly to ecosystem imbalance: when the former advances so does the severity of the latter. Such observations led Hardin to the inevitable conclusion that wanton human breeding is intolerable morally and that freedom in the use of our common property would ultimately bring ruin to us all.

It has been abundantly demonstrated that all interactions between

---

[*]Hardin, Garrett. "The Tragedy of the Commons," *Science* (December 13, 1968), and *Exploring New Ethics for Survival* (New York: Viking Press, 1972).

two or more people begin with an initiator (agent), then evolve into a series of interactive operations between people, finally terminating in a definitive outcome that can be classified as moral or immoral. The criteria of morality are astonishingly simple. All of the foregoing discourse on the ecology of morals can be condensed into the following two statements:

1. A moral act is one in which the agent contributes to and protects the biological requisites and all additional property of self and others without encroaching on the liberty and property of anyone.

2. An immoral act is one in which the agent encroaches on the biological requisites, other property, and the liberty of victims for the purpose of profiting from their losses and without regard for the suffering and harm done to them by the act.

In the above statements the word *act* refers to any interaction between two or more people. The term *agent* stands for the person or persons who initiate the act. *Biological requisites* means any essential organismic need or requirement of a human organism. *Property* refers to both primordial and material property. *Liberty,* as used here, means freedom of movement.

In actuality, the first statement is a summation of ecological moral law, while the second the reciprocal of the first, and hence a derivative thereof, defines the principle underlying immorality.

Statement 1 points out the beneficence of morality. Moral acts are motivated by biological necessity, advantage, and life-enhancement. I have given many examples of biological necessity. The matter of obtaining or being provided with biological necessities is a life-or-death concern. Advantages are tremendously important to the well-being of the organism: e.g., family, employment, skills, education, social organization, freedom from fear, economic scarcity, health, and so on. Certain social characteristics are advantageous, such as friendliness, honesty, fidelity, reliability, and integrity. Life is enhanced by joy and gratification, entertainment, sports and recreation, rest and relaxation, as well as art and beauty. Enhancements could well be as important as necessities and advantages, for without them life could conceivably not be worth living.

It is difficult, if not impossible, to compartmentalize necessities, advantages, and life enhancers. I have sought to compartmentalize as a teaching device and to draw attention to the variety and breadth of moral experience. It is not my intention to suggest that there are different kinds and levels of morality. An act is either moral or immoral for natural reasons, as has been amply illustrated.

What would happen if necessities, advantages, and life enhancers were eliminated? Deprivation of necessities would lead to our extinction. Disadvantageous environmental circumstances would initiate a struggle for existence. The abolition of life enhancements would transform our gratifications and joys in to mere memories.

The second statement impresses us with the degeneracy of immoral behavior. We are brought face to face with an evolutionary holdover, the barbarian or uncivilized human. No one commits a crime because of the nonexistence of alternative methods of acquiring biological necessities. The immorality of crime does not reside in criminals' normal interest in biological necessities, advantages, and life enhancements, but in the threat they pose to the security, well-being, and property of others. An analysis of the moral ecology of crime makes us realize the vast difference in the meaning of "moral" and "immoral."

In statement 2, the agent of an immoral act encroaches on the biological requisites and other property of people, which includes, *ipso facto,* crimes against commonly shared property. Statements 1 and 2 collectively recognize that the agent of an act is influenced by everything that is going on in the ecosystem, by the agent acting in the interest of or to the abuse of the system. People cannot harm the environment without harming the population of that environment. Indeed, morality, to one degree or another, is effected by a multitude of system factors. Hardin's law states simply: "The morality of an act is a function of the state of the system at the time it is performed."* If the production of an ocean fishery is declining (state of the system), would it not be immoral to increase the annual catch, risking the elimination of a valuable economic and food resource? It happened to the sardine industry of Monterey, California. Today tourists visit the ruins of Cannery Row, a monument to immorality.

Here is a way to remember the intent of statements 1 and 2: We are not talking or thinking about morals unless we can relate the subject to:

(1) biological necessity, advantage, and life enhancement, or

(2) an organismic threat coming from the environment, or

(3) an invasion of property rights, including commonly shared property.

---

*Stated in sources noted in footnote on page 156.

An ecology of morals offers a new approach to moral knowledge and authority. Moral ecology vindicates and even reinforces some of the oldest and most common moral concepts and principles, but it does more. It establishes a scientific base for moral knowledge and sets up a measure of morality that is independent from opinion, prejudice, belief, and emotional influence. As world society becomes more interwoven and complex, people everywhere will need to rethink their moral precepts, learning for themselves reliable criteria for making moral judgments. Reliability can be found in the natural laws and principles of moral ecology.

There are no scientifically verifiable theories of the purpose of the universe or of life. We do know that the world and life are set up to run on and on with rather reassuring dependability. Life flow persistently continues from generation to generation against great odds. The biological mechanisms that account for life flow operate, like the universe in general, according to natural law. If human life has a purpose, it is to be found in its genetic program and that man-made construction we call the human ecosystem. Morals are a supportive, structural part of the human ecological program without which all physiological and biochemical processes would ultimately fail.

Morality also is indispensable to civilized behavior. We think of civilization as the fulfillment of humankind's highest potential: the ultimate flowering of human genius. The key discovery that made all others possible is morality and its incorporation into the most complex ecological system as yet devised by a life form. Our human ecology system covers the earth in a vast network of human interactions that are held together and given direction by moral principles that were uncovered during the march of human history. It is no longer acceptable to content ourselves with the theory that moral elements are satisfactorily described as, say, customs, doctrines, sins, conventions, and civil laws. There is a growing body of biological facts and laws that give us a new and simplified view of the nature and function of morality and it has a verifiable scientific foundation.

Part Four is devoted to applications of moral ecology and to the analysis and understanding of a broad range of human behaviors. Our major concern is to help others learn how to be their own moral expert. Subjects have been chosen for study on the basis of their general interest and their usefulness in illustrating the application of moral theory. Detailed and scholarly expositions of the subjects chosen for discussion are beyond the scope of this book.

Part Four
Conquering Moral Problems

21

On Being Our Own Moral Expert

At the beginning of the book, I promised to introduce readers to new moral concepts designed for our times. Further, I promised to provide a practical working knowledge of moral principles that can be used in solving moral problems and dilemmas. This I have done.

Statements 1 and 2 of the preceding chapter are derivatives of the ecological theory of morals set forth in this volume. We shall soon use them in demonstration analyses of a variety of moral problems, particularly those that have fallen heir to muddled thinking. In so doing we shall continue to separate verifiable moral principles from a hodgepodge of feelings, customs, conventions, taboos, sins, laws, and political propaganda that befuddle moral analysis and judgment.

Our task now is to turn theory into practice. Recall Statement 1 and the three notations that infallibly remind us how to recognize when we are talking or thinking about morals:

Statement 1: A moral act is one in which the agent contributes to and protects the biological requisites and all additional property of self and others without encroaching on the liberty and property of anyone.

We can be said to talk or think about morals if we can relate the subject to

1. biological necessity, advantage, and life enhancement, or

2. an organismic threat coming from the environment, or

3. an invasion of property rights, including commonly shared property.

Let's use this statement and the three notations listed above to analyze and describe a series of subjects vital to life in the real world. In other words, we will be discussing applied morality, or morality in action. These subjects are drawn from everyday life and selected for both their general interest and their usefulness. Occasionally we may retrace our steps through subjects that have already been discussed. As we examine each subject, I shall draw attention to the moral ecology implications of the human behaviors involved, and I shall do so by weighing moral and legal judgments against the simple principles of moral ecology.

Behind us lies an exposition of a practical theory of morals based on human nature and human ecology. We have witnessed how the theory was derived from examining anew the facts of our inner environment of self, and the outer environment of other humans and the natural world. I have placed considerable emphasis on how humans have adapted to each other and to their collective habitat. Morals emerge as an adaptive phenomenon, not only for guiding and regulating our relations to each other, but in our uniquely human modification, reformation, and exploitation of our natural surroundings.

LOVE AS MORAL BEHAVIOR

Love is a composite of a number of beneficial adaptations we make to the inner environment of the self and to the outer environment of others. It is one of the most common and essential of our adaptations to the requisites of existence. It parallels our propensity for self-preservation. In fact, love is an essential property of the technology of survival. Like self-preservation, it is a moral imperative.

Similar to so many everyday words, *love* has a variety of meanings, some of them quite trivial. By way of simplification, we shall consider the word love as standing for some kind of action we take with the objective of benefiting ourselves or others. In different words, love is a form of action, not feelings or emotions. The latter, however, may be present as the motivators behind a decision to act. Also, feelings and emotions add color to life, from pain to joy and affection. Despite the psychological importance of feelings and emotions, they have no moral significance in and of themselves. A decision to act out a moral principle may cause us to inhibit a strong emotional impulse.

The psychologist Erich Fromm, in his book *Man For Himself* (1947), made a significant contribution to moral theory, which pointed toward a bioenvironmental theory of morality. Fromm advanced loving as having four phases of action: care, responsibility, respect, and knowledge. Care is used in the sense of a mother caring for her baby. People generally do not take care of something for which they have no responsibility, nor do they tend to assume responsibility for something they do not respect, nor respect something they know nothing about.

Knowledge of the object of our love is the foundation of our ability to love at all. As we come to know someone or something better and better, we may come to respect that individual or thing. The kindling of respect for a person or thing is a factor in our choosing to assume responsibility for either. The quality of our care for the love object is certainly going to be a factor of the strength and depth of our perception of our responsibility for it. The act of caring leads back to increased knowledge and a continuance of what Fromm called the productive love process: knowledge, respect, responsibility, and caring.

Love has just been described as a series of operations (acts) performed by a lover, rather than as the lover's feelings and emotions. The latter have their place in productive love: the lover may suffer pangs of compassion or sorrow in reference to the love object, or experience a gamut of feelings running all the way to elation and joy in being able to serve and benefit the love object. The point here is that feelings and emotions are adjunctive to love, whereas the specific operations with which the lover directly benefits the love object are integral with love. Being operational, love can be regarded as an art requiring many skills. These can be and must be learned. Love is on the highest, most important level of moral activity. It is an ideal expression of the moral principles set forth in Statement 1.

That the word love is used in so many trivial ways makes it difficult to focus on the concept of productive love. The most common trivialization is to use *love* in place of *like, enjoy, prefer, adore, relish, have a fondness for,* and so on, as in such examples as "I love hiking, card games, pets, travel, and gardening." However, if I said "I love rather than like my garden," I could mean love in the productive sense. Caring for a garden could engage my knowledge of horticulture and landscaping; my respect for established gardening practices; my responsibility to apply this knowledge and skill in the planning, planting, and maintenance of it. In pursuing my hobby, I would not encroach on the property rights of others. My accomplishments might be appreciated by others and I would experience some pleasure from success, mixed perhaps with some disappointment at the results of my efforts.

It is not far-fetched to use gardening as an example of productive love. We can truly love an endeavor, a hobby, profession or line of work, and expressions of human creativity and skill. We can love an individual example of human ingenuity, skill, and thought: for instance a great art work, a musical performance, a sports event, a scientific discovery or a technological breakthrough. In such examples we express our love by appreciating, protecting, preserving, and propagating them. Our productive love of the works of nature is manifested in the creation of national parks and monuments.

We can reach an even greater clarification of productive love by contrasting it with romantic love. At the outset we can note that romantic love derives its initial impetus from our joy in meeting or becoming acquainted with someone who strongly appeals to us. This favorable impression increases if we sense in any way that this other person likes us or could come to like us. When we speak of falling in love, we are talking about an unplanned event, like happening to meet somebody who reminds us of an ideal fantasy lover. We may feel excitement and elation like a prospector who has just discovered gold. Our joy can become almost mindless if we feel the other person likes us as much as we like them. Our first impressions can be strengthened as we become better acquainted and discover that we have similar likes and dislikes. Falling in love can evolve into productive love.

As mutual knowledge about each other grows, the stage becomes set for respecting each other, for accepting differences in preferences and opinions, for wanting to help each other obtain personal needs and goals. As a couple we are moving from discovery and knowledge of each other to respect for each other's individuality and, finally, to the affirmation of mutual responsibilities. Mutually helpful caring is at hand. Thus, romantic love has become infused with productive love, a stabilizer without which romantic love will almost certainly be short lived.

In many love affairs, the fact that each partner feels desirable, wanted, and welcome—in a word, loved—by the other, leads each to feel an increased sense of self-esteem and pride. Guilt about past social failures and other shortcomings may be ameliorated or even disappear. This facet of a love relationship can later turn into a psychological minefield, especially in a long-term relationship, where either party through hostile accusations and criticisms may provoke an old feeling of guilt to return in the other, thus weakening or destroying the binding power of productive love.

The durability of romantic love, in the long term, is at risk from the moral failure of one or both of the partners. The chief source of marital failure or the failure of a close relationship is that one or both of the partners are lacking in a knowledge of and skill in productive loving. This predicament is usually the result of the lovers growing up in a setting where productive love was not practiced, where they did not learn about the fruitlessness of adversarial relations, open hostility, vengeful criticism, withdrawal of caring, and broken promises and contracts. People who do not learn even the rudiments of productive love as children may have serious difficulties in social life, work relationships, and sexual functioning in adulthood. They also rarely attain the fulfillment of their potential in any undertaking.

It is important to recognize that there are factors other than ignorance of the art of productive loving that can be held to account for the failure of personal relations and mutual sexual gratification. But continuing the discussion of these factors will only provide us with moral lessons that have already been covered elsewhere in this book.

We have learned that love is a series of actions performed by a lover to benefit another person. Loving involves a series of specific behaviors that not only must be but can be learned. Feelings like compassion are not moral acts, but they may motivate us to care for others. In effectively caring for someone, we must know what to do and how to do it. Additionally, we must want to do it, even though we do not like doing it. Behind our capacity to love productively, we must have knowledge of and experience in productive loving, and we must have accepted the principles of productive love as a central component of our lifestyle.

People whom we regard as mature are likely to have this capacity for productive love. They are the heroes of everyday life who frequently risk all to serve others: they are parents who arise late in the night to comfort a sick child; a physician who struggles to save the life of a murderer; and all people everywhere who serve the welfare of others in social and family life, in a work place, or in an activity as mundane as driving a car.

One of the remarkable things about a loving relationship is that the participants, even in doing something for one another that is distasteful, do not feel or act as though they are making a sacrifice, or being imposed upon in some way. In a truly loving relationship, the intent seems to be to beautify the lives of one another. A loving mother in nursing her baby seems to be enjoying herself, as does the baby; she is not resentful of the situation. Productive love is not being managed correctly if one of the partners behaves as though the labor of caring were a sacrifice of some kind. This kind of situation is common in sexual relations, as every counselor knows. The act of productive love is not only rewarding to the recipient, but to the lover as well. Reciprocity of benefits is a characteristic of human interactions that are governed by ecological moral principles.

The foregoing introduction to productive love presents a brief overview of a few practical behaviors we can personally adopt that meet the demands of Statement 1. The prescription for productive love can be applied to all the interpersonal relationships of everyday life: to those between men and women, men and men, women and women, child and child, adults and children, family members, groups, employers and employees, and, to shorten the list, to every other conceivable type of human interpersonal relationship. Even so, one important relationship remains: it is that of the self to the self. It requires a rather searching scrutiny.

This topic will open to us a very personal, powerful, and necessary dimension of the general subject of becoming our own moral expert. Of course, how we function morally is a factor of how we relate to others. Nonetheless, what we are capable of meaning in the lives of others depends, to a great extent, on the conceptualization of our personal self operating in a world of others. This is what we shall now look into.

THE PROPRIETORSHIP OF THE SELF

We have looked at the operations an individual performs in loving another person. Now we shall examine the operations performed by individuals in loving themselves. This goal demands that we select the most promising place to start the practice of moral ecology, which is caring for our own property. Is there, or should there be, anything more important to us than the care of our own bodies, minds, and derivatives thereof? And who should be responsible for this care if not ourselves?

The ownership of ourselves and all that entails is our business and we are its proprietor. This job is the primary occupation of us all. In general, we do not want our lives managed by others, yet we all too frequently fail to do a capable job of it ourselves. If we desire a profitable life, we must be an excellent proprietor of it. We realize our bodies and minds are the only instruments through which we can experience life. This makes of them our most precious possessions and, therefore, their cultivation and care should be our first priority in the proprietorship of the self.

This view is not an exaltation of selfishness but of enlightened self-interest. Selfishness is a form of immorality, involving the acquisition of personal advantage at the expense of harming or stealing the property of others, or by needlessly, or without rational excuse, depriving another of some relatively insignificant or readily replaceable part of our property. Also, selfishness involves the neglect of social relationships and the general practice of productive love.

Enlightened self-interest is a form of moral activity involving the acquisition of personal advantage. In this case the advantage stems from learning and applying the beneficent injunctions of Statement 1. Enlightened self-interest also involves the spirit and techniques of productive love. For how else can we endow ourselves with greater rewards than to be able to benefit others? We do not look for reciprocity or thankfulness, but for the realization that carefully developed personal strength gives us the means to be worthy of having fellow humans in our lives.

Thus, it is moral to be for the self. This position is a confirmation that we have a foundation for the productive love of the self. If we do not achieve the capability of caring for ourselves, what would give us the confidence, let alone the competence, to care for others? It is well known that the ignorant can teach no one; that the weak cannot help the weak; the blind, the blind; nor the poor feed the starving. Without money, food, or other worldly goods we would have a hard time being a good Samaritan. American society is utterly dependent on those citizens who have gone all out for themselves and who have done this without encroaching on the property of others. These are the people who belong to that company of producers of goods and providers of services who pay taxes and run the country, ostensibly for the welfare of us all. We shall not count in that company frauds, cheaters, and other criminals. Besides squandering our human potentialities, there is no substitute for, nor way out of, learning to become competent proprietors of ourselves—the kind of people who can at least be for themselves without being against anyone.

It is clear that being able proprietors of the self requires that we be for ourselves, that we accept the challenge of making the most we can of ourselves and that we place a high priority on the principles of productive love. Being for the self in no way means that we must be against anyone. To the contrary, it means we must observe the fact that we can best serve our own ends by serving the ends of others. From this angle we see another view of productive love in action. The care of others cannot be neglected without risking a failed proprietorship of the self and the ultimate loss of our own well-being.

When persons give up responsibility for themselves, as sometimes happens in old age, they gradually lose their independence. When the time comes, the experienced proprietor accepts that state of affairs. However, during the major years of life we assume, to varying degrees, many responsibilities for family members, friends, employees, employers, and for the functions of community, institutions, politics, and other associations.

Responsibility for the self means excellent care-taking of the self. We cannot be earnest, honest, and competent in assuming responsibility for others unless we are taking adequate care of ourselves. This moral position is a tough one to construct and maintain. It certainly requires that we not allow ourselves to become slaves of addictive chemical substances, or expose ourselves to dangerous, perhaps fatal, transmittable diseases, or take unnecessary, serious risks of life and limb. It also means learning how to take reasonably good care of the self. If what I am now saying seems a bit moralistic, so be it. However, no one has as yet claimed that it is child's play to become the proprietor of a flourishing business, and becoming a competent proprietor of the business of running our own lives takes some doing. It is not the easiest style of living, but the one that is most apt to succeed in bringing us a rewarding life.

In managing the proprietorship of the self it is simple to avoid immoral behaviors even though both moral and immoral behaviors are products of self-interest. What are the critical differences? (1) Moral behavior allows us to gain our ends without harming or invading the property of others, while (2) immoral behavior requires that we gain our ends by harming and invading the property of others. In example (1), property is transferred legally (by agreement or contract) whereas, in example (2), property is transferred by fraud, theft, or other criminal means. An important step in analyzing a moral problem is to isolate the property factor. Is property being transferred between parties by a mutually satisfying agreement or at the point of a gun? Usually a moral problem is no more complicated than the foregoing example. This can be a great help in managing the self.

Moral behavior does not grow from denying the needs of the self or from extravagant self-sacrifice, but from becoming strong enough to not only support the self but others as well. We come back to loving, our top-rated form of moral action, and can see more clearly that love, as moral behavior, is an extension of the proper and wise love of the self. The art of loving the self and others is the foundation of our commitment to a moral world as epitomized in Statement 1. We cannot rationally expect to live in a moral world without a personal commitment to moral behavior.

In presenting this synopsis of the main elements of a moral proprietorship of the self, I have deliberately skipped over many important, well-known components of a cultured or sophisticated individual. I omitted carving a niche for social conduct (manners and etiquette), for the need to follow our personal interests, for personality and intellectual development, and for personal physical and mental care, all being subjects that have been so broadly covered by the omnipresent self-help books that line the shelves of book stores everywhere.

As we continue our study of applications of ecological moral principles, we shall continue to gather much evidence that Statement 1 is, basically, the framework of both morality and sanity. Does it not seem insane that so many of us work full-time at inventing and employing techniques designed to control and misuse the property of others: their bodies, minds, and other private property? Perhaps sanity and morality are but different conceptualizations of an optimally effective human ecological system. As we move along, we can be looking for signs of this.

MORAL ABERRATIONS IN EVERYDAY LIFE

What are some of the moral ideas and beliefs, values and thoughts of everyday Americans? This is hard information to obtain. Let us see what we can learn from The Great American Value Test, conducted as a TV program in 1979. This unusual program attempted to find the answers to the foregoing questions.* This test was comprised of a mixture of subjects (values) and common moral precepts, eighteen in all. A listing of the items follows in the order of most to least important as ranked by members of the television audience:

1. Family security

2. World peace

3. Freedom

---

*Facts from a write-up of the test in *Psychology Today* (November 1984).

4. Self-respect

5. Happiness

6. Wisdom

7. A sense of accomplishment

8. A comfortable life

9. True friendship

10. Salvation

11. Inner harmony

12. Equality

13. National security

14. Mature love

15. A world of beauty

16. Pleasure

17. An exciting life

18. Social recognition

Our task now is to search each item for evidence of the moral cues mentioned at the beginning of this chapter. I shall begin with the following items: happiness, a sense of accomplishment, a comfortable life, inner harmony, pleasure, an exciting life, and social recognition. The personal conduct that would provide us with the opportunity to have these kinds of experiences can be morally productive and advantageous to a human being and thus moral. If others help us to obtain such advantages, or if we help others have such experiences, this assistance would be credited as moral. However, if any such advantage is procured by encroaching on the prerogatives of others to have similar advantages, the act of so doing would be immoral. These observations are derived from Statements 1 and 2.

Salvation is a religious, doctrinal goal desirable to those who understand and seek it. Equality is an unattainable goal, but the television audience gave it a middle-grade ranking. We wonder what sorts of entities are seen as equal. In human relations, none: in mathematics, many. Wisdom is highly regarded. Who would not want wisdom? It wins a high ranking.

We can say of salvation, equality, and wisdom that there is nothing harmful in holding them out as possibly desirable, if attainable, but they are not moral principles by any measure.

It is hard to understand why mature love received such a low rating. It is a form of action—a specific technology of relating—rather than merely the expression of emotions, and it can be, indeed must be, learned. Mature love is basic to family security and even economic stability might be impossible to achieve without it. I would rate mature love as the most powerful and necessary of all human behaviors, therefore a high-ranking moral concept.

World peace came in ahead of national security. War is unquestionably the greatest of all immoralities. It is no surprise that world peace received a high score. National security is clearly related to family security, yet it received a lower score than the dream state, equality.

The craving for freedom has deep biological roots. Our passion for freedom is as much a part of human nature as our intelligence and our penchant for adherence to beliefs. Our everlasting desire for freedom is an expression of a biological necessity and I class it as a moral imperative. The television audience gave it a high ranking.

Henry David Thoreau, the American naturalist, equated a world of beauty with morality. He felt that to destroy natural beauty was a fatal blow to human welfare and, therefore, immoral. We may soon be wishing we had heeded his words. A world of beauty may not be biologically necessary but it is certainly advantageous and life-enhancing, which classifies it as a moral objective.

The Great American Value Test provides us with eighteen opinions as to what states of mind, life situations, personal preferences, and qualities of life people deem important. The list and rank-ordering provides us with material for moral analysis. Beyond this, we learn from the test that the word *values*, which stands for no particular subject, could not be replaced by *moral, ethical, metaphysical, philosophical,* or any other term. Suffering from illogical subject diversity, the collection of items (values) appears to be muddled.

Before going into additional applications of ecological moral theory, remember that in chapter 2 I abandoned the use of many of the traditional terms of moral discourse. The terms referred to are *good* and *bad, right* and *wrong, good* and *evil, fair* and *unfair, value* and *values, equal* and *equality, virtue* and *vice, justice* and *injustice.* I have written extensively on moral theory and behavior without using these terms. I suggest

174 The Morality Maze

that we continue to improve our thinking about moral matters without falling back on these familiar old terms. The word *ethics,* though fashionable, has also been avoided as much as possible. *Rights* and *freedom* are major moral topics and are given special attention in what follows.

We have just analyzed some American value terms, finding it simple to separate words standing for moral principles (freedom and mature love), religious doctrine (salvation), personal preferences (happiness, pleasure) and favorite values (wealth and an exciting life). Now let us turn our attention to written statements more difficult to evaluate, for example, Mohatma Gandhi's oft quoted seven sins:

1. Wealth without work
2. Pleasure without conscience
3. Knowledge without character
4. Commerce without morality
5. Science without humanity
6. Worship without sacrifice
7. Politics without principle.

Theoretically, each of Gandhi's sins can be classified as a doctrinal taboo or as suggestive of an immoral practice. The Mahatma set them forth as moral guidelines, but they are not phrased as principles. We are not told who is hurt or by whom.

Is the possession of wealth without having worked for it immoral? Not necessarily. If the property were obtained without encroaching on the property of others, its possession would not be immoral. All seven of the sins can be analyzed easily if first we identify the component that represents property. Pleasure is psychological property. Again, if pleasure is experienced without harming the self or others, it is not immoral. If, however, pleasure has been declared sinful, then in the Mahatma's eyes it is just that.

Owning knowledge, like any other property, is not immoral, but it is immoral to use knowledge to harm others. Commerce, or trading property without morality, makes it an immoral activity. Science and politics can be used to benefit or harm people. It is when harm is done that we can agree with Gandhi.

Worship without sacrifice is a baffling abstraction. Worship requires effort, time, and discipline, an expenditure of primordial property. Is more giving and sacrifice required? If so, in what form? We have learned that the cost of loving (in this case, worship) need not be interpreted as sacrifice. This highlights a chronic problem of moral analysis, which is abstraction. In our own discussions of moral issues, we must keep the terms and situational descriptions as specific as possible. If Gandhi was striving to espouse universal moral principles, he chose a rather vague way of making his points. He first writes a noun, which supposedly identifies a kind of property; then he asks us to evaluate its morality in the absence of an important entity, such as work, character, or humanity. Seven sins are listed, but no down-to-earth moral principle is revealed.

Let us now put to further testing what we have learned about morality. In the late twentieth century we are still burdened by many questionable ideas that had their origins in the work of nineteenth-century political and moral philosophers. I am going to describe and analyze several examples of the most influential of these ideas. Some of them have helped erode the very foundations of modern society and civilization: some are still believed by millions even though they contribute to the social and political circumstances that bring about cataclysmic changes throughout the world.

MORAL THOUGHT CAN BE DANGEROUS

The nineteenth century exploded with new moral, political, and social philosophies. In the twentieth century some of these philosophies have actually blown up in our faces, disfiguring the countenance of human experience for all time. Our immediate objective is to become better acquainted with the awesome power of moral ideas, or ideas that pass for moral dicta.

Let us start with a moral concept used by Karl Marx (1818–1883), whose communism spawned violent revolutions and societal changes that directly affected half the population of the Earth. Marx believed that morality is whatever benefited the ruling class at each stage of social evolution. Further, the rules of morality are concocted by the powerful to subordinate and exploit the weak and the poor. Eventually, according to Marx, the communist state would evolve into a classless society in which morality or a code of moral behavior would no longer be needed.

Let us apply to Marx's thoughts our ecologically based moral precepts. We would have to agree that it would be immoral for a ruling class to encroach on the property and biological requisites of an underclass and, further, we would fear that if such behavior were vigorously pursued, it would ultimately threaten to destroy the whole of a society. This appears to be happening today in communist countries, where the ruling circle restricts the biological advantages and life enhancers of the general population, thereby diminishing their work incentives and enthusiasm for supporting costly efforts to spread communism to other countries. Leading communist countries are seeking correctives for excessive exploitation of the nonruling segment of their populations. Marx's ideas about morals are completely at odds with the moral theories presented herein.

Among Marx's most vulnerable concepts is that a classless society will not need morality. No proof of this concept exists because no example of a classless society has as yet emerged. The communist phrase "first among equals" is a blatant advertisement of class distinctions.

The communist state begins with the confiscation of private property and the means of production, the banishment of dissident citizens, and the attainment of underclass cooperation through force. The moral elements of Statement 1 are therefore violated. One cannot imagine a society, classless or otherwise, that would not need the integrative forces of a moral system. Such a society is one in which its parts and functions are synchronized by a behavioral guidance mechanism that regulates and harmonizes all interpersonal transactions (including property transfers) and which, in so doing, reduces destructive conflicts and coercion to the lowest possible level. Even a society of robots would need guidance to protect them from destroying each other. It is not a classless society that people are yearning for; it is the privilege of securing and enjoying their property, which is also the real meaning of freedom (see chapter 23).

Let us move on to some of the moral thoughts of the German philosopher Friedrich W. Nietzsche (1844-1900), who suggested that human evolution is moving toward production of a dominating superman. He wanted humankind to look beyond good and evil in order to release its natural "will to power." Nietzsche's life ended when Adolf Hitler was but a boy. Little evidence exists to support a theory that Hitler and the Nazis were markedly influenced by Nietzsche's writings, however, the philosopher's work was interpreted by some Nazis to justify their goals. It is a quirk of history that Hitler, in many ways, was erroneously regarded as a fulfillment of Nietzsche's ideal; the superman who would conquer and make over the world. However, Hitler attempted to do just that. Part of his plan was the provocation of World War II, the most destructive and costly military conflict in history.

Now, functioning as our own moral experts, what we discern here is a philosophy of force and power (domination) and a need to brush aside conventional morality (good and evil) which now liberates the leader to commit any immorality for the sake of victory. Hitler's Nazi movement thus became the epitome of ecological immorality.

Nietzsche saw morality (ethics) as a hindrance to the further development of society and as being a device invented by the weak to subdue the strong. While history records no example of the weak suppressing the strong, it is interesting to note that Marx expressed the opposite opinion —that morals were invented by the rich and powerful to subdue the weak and to justify their subservience and exploitation. We wonder how these two men, among the brightest of their era, arrived at opposite and erroneous views on the etiology of morals. This matter alone invites us to re-examine the veracity of all they had to say. This we know: the two stimulated wave after wave of unprecedented violence and societal change.

Marx and Nietzsche justified their social and political objectives on the basis of vastly different moral codes. Nevertheless, their interpreters led the world from one disaster to another, proving that unexamined moral theorizing can have dangerous consequences. Their lives and work, also, prove that good intentions do not ameliorate immoral outcomes.

It would be hard to find more striking examples of the dangers of moral theorizing than the two we have just studied. However, other concepts, construed as having moral value, emerged in the nineteenth century and possess to this day popular acceptance and acclaim. A few examples follow.

Let us first consider majority rule. Our electoral system evolved in the nineteenth century to nearly its present form. A basic premise of the system is majoritarian government. An elective public office is won by the candidate who receives a majority of the votes of the electorate. The same principle holds for the passage of a law by a legislative body, or for the qualifying of a referendum or initiative placed before the voters.

The danger of our electoral system is that it can produce a tyranny of the majority. However, in a democracy majority rule practically eliminates the possibility of establishing a tyranny of the minority. Aside from this point, not many arguments can be advanced to show that majority rule makes a society safer or more effective than would minority rule. Majority rule is likely to be ineffective about fifty percent of the time. A dictatorial majority could legally control the other side indefinitely through various forms of coercion, thus opening a way to encroach on the primordial and other properties of a minority, which could result in the practice of intolerable immorality. Any form of tyranny, whether of a minority or of a majority, can be harmful to a human ecosystem. Probably no law should be passed solely on the basis of the number favoring it, but only on the basis of its morality in an ecological sense. We must provide a test more reliable than opinion. I suggest using the simple principles revealed by moral ecology.

Many people today believe that a society should dedicate itself to doing "the greatest good for the greatest number." This concept was conceived by Jeremy Bentham (1748-1892), and elaborated by John Stuart Mill in *Utilitarianism* (1863). Mill believed that everyone should act for the good of the greatest number. This is an excellent example of juggling abstractions. Whose definition of "good" is to be accepted? The phrase "greatest number" brings to mind our distrust of the infallibility of the wisdom of majority decisions.

One fundamental moral injunction emerged from the nineteenth century: the moral worth of an act depends on one's motive or intention, not on outcomes. An act motivated by the best of intentions may turn out to be immoral. Is the actor then immoral? A human ecosystem cannot flourish on harmful input whether blameworthy or not. Morals in an ecological system are tied to consequences. Investigative and legal work requires inquiry into motives, but moral analysis does not. It is concerned only with consequences. Even though we are ignorant of moral culture, we can still commit an immoral act. We do not have to know an act will cause harm to others for it to be regarded as immoral. An act is not amoral to those who are harmed by it. Behavior damaging to the ecosystem is immoral whether or not it was intentional.

Throughout this book, I have often called attention to words and phrases that tend to confuse issues and muddle thinking about morals. None are more troublesome than the most everyday, commonly used political terms: republic, democracy, conservative, liberal, rights, freedom, and equality. A brief critique of each term follows.

Republic and *democracy* are virtually synonymous. They both stand for rule by the public, rule by law, majority rule, rule by elected representatives, the (supposed) equality of all before the law (all citizens being treated equally by the government), and equality of opportunity. The titular head of a republic is elected, not a monarch, as may be true in a democracy. Strictly speaking we should call the United States government a republic because all our representatives are elected by the people, but it is traditional, though technically incorrect, to speak of our country as a democracy. We have a penchant for using words for effect and for engineering consent, not for the sake of accurate communication.

Conservative and *liberal,* in an American political sense, can be regarded as antonyms. Conservatives usually stand for the preservation of traditions and institutions. They tend to be moderate and prudent in spending public money on extensive social programs. Conservatives are often members of the Republican party though this is not a binding rule. Neither Republicans or Democrats can boast of being least fraudulent or most ethical.

The word *liberal* means, literally translated from the Latin, "for freedom." As often used, this word is a flagrant misnomer. Democrats label themselves liberal. Neither party earned this label because neither specifically work to advance freedom (see chapter 23). The callous disregard of the true meaning of liberal is dangerous to democratic and moral government.

Embedded deeply in democratic thought are the ideas of majority rule, representative government, equality, fairness, rights and freedom. These factors are the basis of the great morality game of American politics. All games have rules, and any deviation from the set rules brings on a cry that one is unfair. Issues are supposedly fairly and squarely decided on the basis of majority rule, but if a legislative decision is accused of favoring a minority group, it is immediately declared unfair. If it veers from the mythical idea of equality for all, it is unfair. If it asks for more sacrifice by one group of taxpayers than another, it is labeled unfair. Politically, we want to avoid the "unfair" label. We are cautious about being accused of discrimination, i.e., favoring one group rather than another on the basis of color, sex, health, religion, country of origin, physical handicaps, and so on. There are many difficulties in the unfairness of majority rule; discriminating against minority parties frequently deprives their members of rights. The struggle for equality, if it were carried out in a systematic way, would ultimately reduce the whole population to the same dead level of mediocrity. Behind the search for fairness is the search for equality. Little by little the American people are being trained to think that equality is not only possible, but that it is, or should be, the destiny of democracy.

Do Americans really want total and complete equality? We do not want equality of all individual differences and characteristics. Who wants to be on a par with an infant, the aged, the diseased, the insane, the dope addict, the criminal, a man waiting on death row? What we want is an unearned share of the other guy's wealth, good fortune, material property! We want a part of the winnings of our neighbors who are better or luckier players than we at the game of life. If these were our goals, would we be following the dictates of Statement 1 or Statement 2?

Are we truly a government of the governed? This question is a reflection of an underlying theory of representative government. We cannot prove that we have ever had a political system that is truly representative of the electorate.

Freedom can and should be similar for all, but this does not imply that it gives us a right to force others to accept absolute equality. Society is not morally obliged to divide property according to some preconceived formula or law. Nature provides no such guarantee that, for example, every child will be born with a brain. Biology does not require the impossible, namely equality. Our attempts to make up for the discrepancies of nature can have qualitatively mixed results: increasing athletic prowess with hormones, for example. A race of clones would be the ultimate equality, but do we want equality or just a bigger slice of the other guy's pie?

The German philosopher Georg Hegel (1770–1831) was busy inventing his theory of the supremacy of the state while his contemporary in the New World, George Washington, was helping the newly established United States to become the first successful democracy, a country whose government would be subservient to the wishes and demands of the people. Hegel believed that the state, like an organism, has an existence and purpose above and beyond those of its constituent parts. The state has a life of its own. The lay citizen's duty is to serve and support the state, but not to direct or manage it. The state had unlimited power to direct its destiny. Unlike Hegel's ideal system, the United States established a form of government that rather effectively controls the power of government. The separation of powers into the executive, the legislative, and the judiciary provides a constant check on excess and abuse of authority. We seemed never to have regarded the government as better equipped to run the country than the people themselves. When individual citizens become less important than government, freedom is gone.

The ideal state, according to Hegel, would be a monarchy governed by a constitution. The protection of the citizens and their property would be guaranteed by law. The success of states would be judged by their ability to win wars. The purposes, intentions, and determinations of the state, the "common will," would somehow be expressed through the behavior of the state. We can well imagine that Nietzsche and Hitler found inspiration in Hegel. The political philosophy of Hegel is now referred to as statism. It is still alive and healthy. Millions of us continue to believe that government can be all, know all, and do all, and, worse yet, spend our money with more wisdom than we can.

Until quite recently Americans generally thought of the state as an instrument designed to carry out the will of the people. Now they are beginning to wonder if this is still so. Our government appears to be changing: particularly the legislative branch, which is becoming separated from the ordinary citizen. More and more people are feeling denied a say in how they are governed. Congress is not renewing itself. Members seem virtually settled in their jobs for life. We seldom see new faces in Congress. Are we moving from government of, by, and for the people to an oligarchy whose members have tenure for life? We should be seriously concerned when individual citizens become less important to the state than the state's social and economic plans for the individual. The plan, not people, is the focus of statism. The combination of expensive social programs and the way we go about funding them entangles us in four immoralities: profligacy, fraud, subterfuge, and diminution of freedom.

It is so easy for those who manage a state, whether elected by the people or self-appointed dictators, to perceive themselves as the rulers, rather than as the servants of the people. We should listen to them, albeit cautiously, but we do not need to believe them. The role of being our own moral expert requires constant vigilance regarding wayward and high-sounding ethical and moral assertions, principles, ideas, values, and opinions.

OBJECTIVE VERSUS RELATIVE MORALS

Most people are familiar with the erroneous idea that morals are relative. The moral principles based on human ecology are derived from the natural laws of human biology, not from the comparative history of various social conventions, civil laws, religious doctrines, and philosophical speculations. In the foregoing text, we have learned that an ecological science of morals reveals that moral laws are objective and universal (transcultural).

Many of us use the term *moral value*, but regardless of what is meant by *moral*, the addition of *value* is confusing and adds a note of uncertainty. The combination means nothing and should be abandoned for the sake of clarity.

Basic moral principles are objective and shared by all humans. What changes is the ecosystem. An established moral principle is not replaced, it is simply eclipsed, sometimes totally and for long periods of time. The dependable reference point for determining the moral status of a behavior is organismic necessity. When an ecosystem crisis subsides, an eclipsed moral principle returns to dominance. Let's introduce an example of a moral eclipse in the context of a current ecosystem crisis.

In the 1970s there was a widespread, unconcealed rejection of long-standing sexual conventions and laws, respecting homosexuality and extra-marital heterosexuality. Lovers of both persuasions came out in the open and demanded and obtained a considerable measure of social acceptance and legal standing. The 1970s also witnessed an alarming increase in sexually transmitted diseases (STDs), which was capped in the 1980s by AIDS. The benefits of sex hygiene and monogamous sexual relationships were rediscovered. AIDS evoked the dictum that its spread by any means is the moral equivalent of murder. Thus, a new sexual moral code eclipsed an old one, which, in the future, will probably return when the AIDS epidemic has been conquered.

In the future, sexually transmitted diseases will be a thing of the past and birth control technology will have been perfected. Huxley's *Brave New World* goes further than this, picturing state nurseries where babies are grown in artificial wombs, thus, apparently, delivering women from the burden of pregnancy. In Huxley's world there would be little need for sexual restraint between consenting persons of any age or sexual persuasion. All sexual behaviors would be moral. Sexual abuse of children, rape, and other property transgressions would be forbidden for reasons other than the sexual considerations. Thus we can imagine a time when the sexual moral code of the AIDS era will move on and the free-for-all sexual morals of the 1960s will come out from under a long eclipse. A basic moral principle is not arbitrary and relative but stands as a remnant of the ecosystem state that gave rise to it.

CONTRACTS, AGREEMENTS, AND PROMISES

Whether written or verbal, contracts, agreements, and promises are among the most important moral devices in the whole range of human relations reaching across society: from constitutions and business articles of incorporation to marriage vows and the keeping of social appointments. Treaties are but contracts between nations and their violation is a serious matter.

The unilateral breaking of an agreement or a promise can cause untold psychological harm and property loss. If you want to scar the psyche of a child, break a promise. If you want to damage a marriage, break the vow of sexual fidelity. Elected officials who fail to keep their promises destroy their constituents' faith in government. Adolf Hitler's utter rejection of international treaties led to a war that took ninety million lives. The breach of corporate covenants can degrade the life savings and health of hundreds of stockholders.

The failure to keep contracts, agreements, promises, and treaties is immoral. In some cases the damage of such failure has painful consequences. The creative work of the world rides on the meticulous carrying out of agreements and promises by people whom we come to praise for their honesty, trustworthiness, integrity, and other qualities we associate with dependable character.

It is so easy to neglect fulfilling a promise, and after having caused someone great disappointment, it is so easy to apologize. Breaking even verbal contracts tells people you are unconcerned with the integrity of their property. Civilization manages to stay on track thanks to the fact that most of the parties to contracts fulfill their agreements and promises. Great social and individual harm is done by the breaking of promises, agreements, and contracts. This is a source of the most common form of immorality in American life.

Everyday we buy and sell property. We also make and receive gifts of property. The rendering of services is also property. Irrespective of the size of the deal, a property transfer involves contracts, agreements, and promises. To make this specific I have listed below several examples of moral and immoral property transfers, using the principles of moral ecology.

Examples of moral property transfers:

1. any giving of personal property to others (services, love, money, goods, etc.);

2. any rendering of services to others for a contracted fee or wage;

3. any trading relationship with others that is freely entered; and

4. any trade we make for profit that does not encroach on the property or liberty of others.

Examples of immoral property transfers:

1. any services or material property of others that is obtained by force, threats, coercion, or false promises, or the use thereof;
2. any failure to recompense others for contracted services and property purchase agreements;
3. any transaction employing the subjugation of others: e.g., blackmail, hostage-taking, kidnaping, etc.;
4. any profit-making act that invades the property rights of others: e.g., armed robbery, murder, environmental pollution, etc.

A contract faithfully fulfilled is a reliable route to a long-term gain. The breaking of a vow, promise, contract, or agreement is immoral because usually it places a short-term, selfish gain ahead of long-term gain and other persons may be hurt in the process. Affairs, broken promises, and contracts are accompanied by other immoralities such as cheating, dishonesty, fraud, betrayal, scandal, desertion, physical or emotional abuse, stealing, and noncompensation. There is a moral and legal way to break contracts and agreements: first, serve notice that you are going to do it; second, give all partners their freedom from the contract; and third, compensate all partners for material losses your decision caused.

Everyone entering a contract should prepare at the time it is made for the eventuality that a party to the contract may elect to break it. The process for breaking or withdrawing from a contract should be provided at the time it is drawn. No one should enter a contract they are not certain they can fulfill.

CONFLICT

Conflict between individuals or groups can present the moral analysts with serious problems until they realize that conflict is not invariably an immoral phenomenon. Until a disagreement breaks into a quarrel, wherein the property rights of adversaries are threatened, no immorality has occurred. Conflict, however, brings with it the possibility of escalating into a furious, even deadly contest.

Differences of opinions, goals, ethnic identity, social class, religious views, and political affiliations can ignite a conflict. Our perceptions of the behavior of others as being, say, over-demanding, insulting, belittling, dishonest, and so on can also trigger conflict. Ideas are personal property and are subject to appropriation and ridicule by others. Such acts can be interpreted as threats and become grounds for conflict. As we've seen, a frequent cause of conflict is the breaking of contracts, agreements, and promises.

Pages could be filled with examples of conflict ranging from international warfare to a lovers' quarrel. A common manifestation of conflict is factional political controversy and dissentions, from the seats of the mighty to the demonstrations of grassroots activists. Conflict, or awareness of conflict, is a part of everyday life. We all tend to fight for our beliefs and for what we need and want. This brings us into conflict with those whose beliefs, needs, and wants are at variance with our own. Conflicts have also arisen from oppression. A familiar example is the American Revolutionary War, which was waged to free the colonies from the abusive and arbitrary administration of the British Empire. Islamic holy wars and the catholic and protestant hostilities in Northern Ireland will remind us of the hundreds of religious conflicts that bedeck world history.

Conflict can erupt into the irrevocable violence of war in which the adversaries are locked by their respective passions to the end where one or the other, or both go down in defeat. All wars have an initiating agent. In moral ecology, wars can be reduced to the conflict between a threatening agent on the one hand and the victim's struggle to exist or prevail on the other. Probably throughout history, but certainly in the twentieth century, no wars were really won. Even the principles for which we fought are rapidly fading from the collective consciousness of the living.

Statements 1 and 2 fully explain how morality can be assessed in all cases of conflict. In making assessments we must remember that not all conflicts are immoral. We must also remember that some conflicts escalate into the realm of irrational and psychotic behavior. Some of the wild and barbaric outcomes of conflict are explicable on the basis of aberrant biological functioning for which there may be no available remedy. Cataclysmic conflicts run their course. Like hurricanes and volcanic upheavals, they exceed our present capacity to prevent and control them. History reveals that moral remonstrance has been ineffective in ameliorating or ending large-scale conflicts such as war. International efforts during the Iran-Iraq War are an example.

The destruction of human life and habitat by natural forces beyond human control is obviously in a nonmoral dimension of reality. Occasionally, human conflict can rise to a level of irrationality that resembles a natural disaster in progress. Such a predicament, like the aftermath of an earthquake, is irreversible. The difference is that the man-made catastrophe is preventable. The moral dilemmas of war are embedded in the enigmas of conflict prevention, not in the horrors of battle.

COMPETITION

Competition is closely related to conflict. We are most apt to be out to win for ourselves, our side, and our beliefs. We have learned that to profit from life is moral, but not if it requires us to encroach on the property of others. When we fail to observe this principle we invite conflict. Conflict is often a function of competition that ruptures the boundaries of others' property prerogatives. Competition draws on organismic survival mechanisms that energize conflict. The will to not only win (survive), but to prevail is the essence of sports, games, and competitive enterprises.

COOPERATION

Cooperation is not so much an alternative to competition as it is a part of the technique of competing. In team games and enterprises of all kinds, successful competition demands the cooperation of team members. The best players in a game cannot win without cooperative team support.

Creative cooperation is what two or more people decide to do together to produce a mutual profit. Cooperation and competition, however, have no particular moral connotation. Criminals can cooperate with one another, compete, or get into conflicts over territory or the division of spoils. The function of cooperation is group profit.

Humankind reached a point long ago when games substituted for destructive forms of conflict. The role of competition in human ecology keeps changing its character. It has less and less to do directly with survival. Games are the cultural remnants of an ancient moral need for conflict and power. The threat of nuclear war is a new experience for humanity. We have no information based on the experience of having fought a nuclear war, and many doubt that an all-out nuclear confrontation can be won by any combatant. We may be at one of those extraordinary junctures in history where an old standby like competition will be partially, if not totally, eclipsed by cooperation. Competition stands rather nervously at the crossroads of morality, awaiting not its demise but a signal to yield more ground to cooperation.

Moral ecology offers a well known, simple strategy for the control of conflict: prevention. At first glance this appears overly simple, even childish; however, all moral law reflects elementary biological facts that can be understood by children. The prevention of catastrophic conflict is an absolute biological necessity. It ranks at the top of the list of biological necessities along with having adequate nutrition and shelter, caring and being cared for, preserving our property rights, and protecting our common habitat.

The basic operational mechanisms of conflict prevention are cooperation and competition, in that order. Imagine the Soviet and American peoples and their leaders engaged in a cooperative war on war. They could vigorously compete at this game because at the point when both sides decide to end it, they would both be winners. War, the single greatest enemy of human ecology, would have been vanquished. This would increase our chance of wiping out other ecological enemies, such as overpopulation and environmental despoliation. There is no way to dodge scientifically verifiable natural principles. We must acknowledge and obey them or perish. The moral guidelines set forth in Statements 1 and 2 were derived from scientific facts.

This chapter has been dedicated to demonstrating the use of moral ecology principles in describing and analyzing the moral factors embedded in a variety of usual and unusual human interactions and predicaments. This has been offered as instruction on ways to apply what we have learned about the functions of morality in human interrelationships. We could go on with this process, analyzing a seemingly endless number of important problems, issues, and dilemmas. But to do so would change the direction of this book from an illustrated exposition of an ecological theory of morals to a series of commentaries on the probable causes and cures of the ills of the world.

The last two chapters, on rights and freedom respectively, lead us through the most befuddling and exasperating zones of the morality maze. They will provide further insights and sharpen the skills of those who have yet to be their own moral expert. We can go on, then, to find pleasure and benefits in testing our own skills at moral analysis on the great social, economic, and political problems of the day.

22

Rights

Right(s) has become one of the most overworked and least understood words in both conversation and the media. We are bombarded with the word from every direction: the right to work, the right to housing, the right to personal protection, children's rights, animal rights, fetal rights, health-care rights, the right to privacy, the right to know, and on and on. Then come rights to freedom from this or that: freedom from want, from fear, from poverty, from arbitrary job dismissal, from sexual harassment, and so on. Even the rights of rivers to travel to the sea unrestrained by human activity have been proclaimed.

Our clamor for rights is accompanied by a powerful hunger to cash in on all the rights to which we are entitled by law. Besides, we put pressure on lawmakers to bless all our other proclaimed rights with the sanctity and force of law. Lawmakers oblige us by turning our dreams into laws. In 1989, California legislators passed, and the governor signed into law, about 1,500 new pieces of legislation. Imagine the total new 1989 laws for the whole United States: federal, state, county, city, and village! Very likely, tens of thousands of laws are created per year. It is difficult for us ordinary citizens to keep tabs on them. Despite the plethora of new laws, rights activist groups press on and sometimes, in their zeal, demonstrate indifference to laws, common decency, and manners. We witness this in the uncompromising and acrimonious attacks on birth control clinics and animal research laboratories by fetal rights and animal rights activists.

In furthering our development of expertise in moral analysis, we now turn to a careful examination of the word *right(s)*. This will involve learning its different meanings and when and how to use or omit using it in moral discussions.

The first thing we might note is that we have no evidence of the existence of natural or God-given rights. If such rights do exist, then life could not be terminated in any way. Life would come to us with an irreversible guarantee against death. We know this is not the case. The plain facts are that we have no natural right to life, to freedom, to food and drink, to warmth and comfort; no right to be loved; and no right to own our primordial being. All rights to these things and to the use of our common property, the biotic and abiotic environment, referred to in chapters 14, 15, and 16, are man-made. The right to life, for example, is a legal concept. No biologically based right to life exists. A right is conferred by man-made law, not nature. We have the right to life to the extent that the law-enforcement powers of government can guarantee it, which, along with self defense, are extremely limited. Our task now is to put order and rationality into the discussion of rights.

A distinction is sometimes made between *civil liberties* and *rights* in a more general sense. The Fourth Amendment to the United States Constitution, which protects us "against unreasonable searches and seizures" by government agents, is an example of a civil liberty. When a law confers upon us permission to behave in a certain way, it is usually termed a *right* and the First Amendment offers five examples.* The term *civil rights* is frequently used to describe the rights of minorities to have the same privileges that are accorded to other citizens. In the discussion that follows, rights are examined from the viewpoint of ecologically based moral theory. This leads to some rights definitions that are at variance with conventional treatments of the subject.

The word *right(s)* comes with a profusion of definitions and common usages. For example, rights may mean in accordance with justice, law, morality; or it may mean to be correct, to have the right answers; or to put things in order, to set to rights; or to make right by avenging a wrong. It seems that meanings and usages go on endlessly: right hand, right side, feel right, right about face, right minded, right wing, and so on.

---

*Our Constitution permits or allows us to take part or not take part in the establishment or practice of a religion; to speak or publish what we wish; to assemble publicly for a lawful purpose; and to openly criticize actions of our government.

LEGAL RIGHTS

A right can be defined as a power or privilege that belongs to a person by law. Rights are granted or conferred by governments. They are matters of law and should be designated as *legal rights* to distinguish this special use of the word *right(s)* from all its other uses. Each individual right must be established by law. To have any substance in reality, legal rights must be enforceable by the state's police powers, the courts of law, and the penal codes and institutions of government. Just as a product guarantee is no more dependable than the company that made it, so a legal right is no more substantive than the government that granted it.

Only government, irrespective of its structure and quality, has the authority to establish, confer, grant, give, and bestow legal rights.* In the United States a legal right says that certain behaviors are sanctioned by the body politic. A legal right simply permits or allows us to do certain things. Our individual states also confer legal rights. They regularly qualify candidates for many vocations and professions by licensing, certifying, and registering successful candidates; such persons have no legal right to offer their services for wages or fees without possessing the special permit. Even driving a car requires a special license or permit. The license to drive is said to be a privilege, not a right. All license or privilege to drive that is conferred by law is equivalent to a right. Qualifications for licensing can be upgraded from time to time. Licenses, like all other legal rights, are subject to revocation.

Legal rights are generally as stable as other laws. Yet our security in them extends no farther than the enforcement ability of the state. State-conferred rights also are subject to alteration and elimination. An example is the current legal right of women to choose abortion if they so wish. The U.S. Supreme Court can reverse this right, thus making abortion a crime. We must fight to win and then fight again to maintain each specific legal right. This should make us realize again that no known rights are permanent.

---

*Some religions favor a view that doctrinal principles and the laws of God, as stated in sacred documents, take precedence over human laws. Religion has had varying degrees of influence over lawmakers for thousands of years. In America, our diversity as a people and our constitution has blocked any specific religious institutions from dominating the legislative process. However, in 1989, five conservative Supreme Court justices took an essentially anti-abortion stand based primarily on conventional Christian moral precepts, thus seemingly ignoring the doctrine of separation of church and state.

During the Reagan presidency the rights of the unborn became a prominent issue. A constitutional amendment was proposed that would confer on a fetus the right to life, in other words, the right to be carried by its mother to parturition and viable babyhood. Probably as many as one-third of our population support the creation of legal rights for fetuses. As yet such a legal right does not exist. This illustrates the difference between a declaration of rights and a legal right. Anyone can declare or proclaim a right, but it takes some doing to set in motion the processes for creating a legal right. The Declaration of Independence is our most important example of a declaration of rights, but we had to fight a revolutionary war to establish our legal right to independence from England.

A few simple but popular legal rights exist that are backed by constitutionally based common law. For instance, if I loan my car to a friend for a day, on the day of use my friend has a legal right to drive my car. We regularly loan our cars, clothes, tools, and other things to friends and neighbors. These property loans imply that the borrowers have a legal right to use our property within the confines of a possible verbal agreement. When we loan, make a gift, or rent property, we, in effect, grant a right to use the property. The terms of rental agreements are usually written. When we accept a gift, we take for granted that we now have the legal right to own it.

In addition to legal rights, we witness three other species of rights: wish-list rights, self-conferred rights, and a large formalized body of rights known as human rights. I shall briefly describe each.

WISH-LIST RIGHTS

Wish-list rights are the most common variety of believed-in rights. It is a matter of style today, in talking about desires and wishes for possible future laws, to use the words *right to* as in "Everyone should have a right to employment, good wages, decent housing, crime-free streets, and free job training," instead of "I wish everyone could have employment, good wages, decent housing, etc." This common use of the words *right to* merely makes a statement of our wishes, hence the label "wish-list rights." The word *right* is part of the wish, for our chief way of making the wish come true is to make it a legal right. This, then, demands that government do the wish-fulfilling job and that somebody other than the wisher pay for it.

Many wish-list rights statements are trivial. Some are even socially dangerous. An example that is both trivial and untrue might be "Every child has a right to be loved." No government could enforce the right to be loved. This can easily be changed to a true statement: "Children benefit from being loved."

The legalization of some rights proposals could endanger the stability and well-being of society. It costs a lot of money and effort to convert a rights proposal into law and a lot more of both to enforce it. Promoters of rights frequently ignore or do not know the ultimate economic, political, and social costs of the laws they seek to establish. Right-to-life activists are a good example. If they are successful, over a million abortions performed each year on poor women will not take place. Much of the burden of supporting the unwanted infants will have to be carried by the general public. No assurance is offered that a significant percentage of these infants will be adopted. The cost of public assistance in raising a million children to adulthood (eighteen years of age), according to one Kansas state legislator, could run as high as 205 billion dollars, based on a cost of 205 thousand dollars per child.* Anti-abortionists have not presented a plan to pay for the probable enormous expense of their proposal, which would advance geometrically year after year.

As we listen to the daily litany of rights proposals, we become aware that rights advocates want all of their objectives, but not at their own expense. It is important to remember that a rights proclamation can be translated into a declaration of wants, desires, hopes, longings, and aspirations. This is the point to begin analyzing the morality of a particular rights proposal. I find it helpful to avoid the use of wish-list rights phrases when communicating about moral issues. I have done so in this book, using the word *right(s)* only in the sense of legal rights, except, of course, in this chapter.

We wonder how long the number of wish-list rights can keep growing. It is moral that we should establish legal rights to the necessities of biological existence. Beyond that, how far should we go in building a lawyer's world of rights without imposing rational limits? The time has come to swing from our preoccupation with rights to a similar degree of concentration on our responsibilities.

Let us interrupt our wish-list rights analysis and direct attention to our responsibilities to the totality of our ecosystem: to preserving and even

---

*See Ellen Goodman "A Lock on the Womb," *Santa Rosa Press Democrat* (February 19, 1991).

improving the inhabitability of our planet. As moral experts, we must prepare ourselves for the inevitable: the day when we shall be forced to shift our sights from rights to the necessity of protecting our environment. As people and their governments are driven by circumstances to shift their focus from rights to responsibilities, the climate for the moral development of society will improve.

Before World War II the daily news commonly carried articles recommending new laws. If enough people opposed reckless driving, business fraud, political graft, alcoholism, littering, kidnaping, and other socially harmful behaviors, laws were created to prohibit them. Even though such a strategy did not reverse immorality, faith in the saying "there ought to be a law . . ." remained popular. This phrase has now been replaced by "we ought to have a right to. . . ." The familiar result is the continuous stream of rights pronouncements: the wish lists of individuals and groups seeking special privileges, entitlements, services, economic aid, health insurance, and the like through governmental intervention. The old "We need a law to stamp out irresponsible behavior" has changed to "We demand of government the right to have the fulfillment of our wishes."

With the rise of serious environmental problems, we may soon be pressed by life-threatening circumstances to go all out for the creation of laws designed to suppress activities harmful to vital components of the human ecosystem. Thus, at the end of this century, we may find the clamor for rights being changed back to a clamor for prohibitions.

SELF-CONFERRED RIGHTS

When we make a decision and act on that decision, we have, in effect, conferred a specific right upon ourselves. This is exactly what we do many times every day: We permit all of our own behaviors and, thus, are solely responsible for their moral and legal outcomes. The formula of a self-conferred right is practically identical to that of a simple decision.

First, we have a desire to act (motivation), illustrated by a sentence like "I am hungry and I want to eat." Hunger is the motivation, while "I want to eat" is the expression of a desire. The next step could be expressed by the sentence "I want to eat now," which indicates that the decision to eat has been made. The sentence "I am eating" points out that the decision is now being acted upon.

The kinds of decisions we make can be moral or immoral. If in acting out a decision we encroach on the property of others, we have embarked on an immoral course. The variety of decisions leading to some kind of action seems endless. We may decide to purchase a business, to get married, to have children, to change jobs, to rob a bank, to kill for hire, to commit suicide, and so on. The decisions we make can be moral or immoral, legal or illegal. Each personal decision acted upon can be termed a self-conferred right. An example: teenagers who claim they have a right to sex.

Everything we are by nature, experience, and education becomes, at one time or another, involved in our decision-making process. Decision making, no matter how simple, can defy analysis and the accurate delineation of motivation. For example, muggers occasionally shoot victims. The etiology of the impulse to murder a victim may not be as simple as theorizing that the killer merely wanted to avoid the chance of being identified by his victim. The psychological analysis of even a simple decision can be complex. However, moral analysis of a decision's outcome is simple by comparison. All we need to know is if the decision maker transgressed the primordial and material property of others. The evidence we look for is harm to primordial property and adverse effects on material property. These suggestions give us something definite and concrete to consider in the process of making a moral judgment. Also, this is one more illustration of how simple it is to make moral judgments based on the findings of moral ecology.

HUMAN RIGHTS

Usually the words *human rights*,* as employed here, refer to legal rights and rights proposals (wish-list rights) designed to protect the life, liberty, and other properties of citizens from encroachment by government and other sources of power and authority. As with laws in general, human rights are no more secure and dependable than the authority that grants and guarantees them. The concept of human rights requires that government voluntarily limit its authority. This puts certain prerogatives of citizens above those of government. The United States Constitution actually declares that the power and authority of the people are above those of

---

*Custom is probably the reason for adopting the term. The word *human* adds no special meaning to the discussion of rights. The term seems to be but a mere label for a group of important legal and proposed rights; the United Nations Universal Declaration of Human Rights has most likely cemented these words together permanently.

the government. The first ten amendments to the Constitution (The Bill of Rights, 1791) conferred on the people a string of behavioral prerogatives and primordial and material property protections that, collectively, were a new thing in the world. They described what the government would not prevent us from doing and what the government would do to protect our interests as individuals. This, basically, is what human rights are all about.

The early American authors of the Declaration of Independence and the Constitution believed in inalienable rights, which we should not and, ultimately, cannot be denied by our fellow humans. In the seventeenth century, human rights came to be regarded as representing "higher law" or "natural law." Such ideas were published in France under the title of The Declaration of the Rights of Man and of the Citizen (1789), which called for the guarantee of liberty, property, security, freedom of speech, freedom of the press, and abolition of oppression. Human-rights formulations are expressions of moral law. Generally, they measure up to the criteria of morality found at the end of chapter 20, which are derived from facts of human biology. These, of course, can be said to be inalienable.

In 1988, the United States Constitution contained twenty-six amendments, eighteen of which deal with human rights, often referred to as civil rights and liberties. Also, the term *civil rights* is, erroneously, thought of as just a label for minority rights. Taken collectively, civil rights and civil liberties cover practically every statute from freedom of speech to criminal law.

On December 10, 1948, the United Nations General Assembly adopted the Universal Declaration of Human Rights, consisting of thirty articles ranging from the safeguarding of life and liberty to the abolition of oppression, torture, and slavery. The fortieth anniversary of this famous document was celebrated December 10, 1988. On this day, according to news reports, moral trouble spots existed throughout the world. Paraguayan police, for example, attacked hundreds of people at Asunción to prevent a march to commemorate the day. Failure to observe and enforce the Universal Declaration remains worldwide.

The above declarations of human rights are especially remarkable for their overriding purpose, which is the compilation of moral behaviors and principles that will ultimately serve all the peoples of the Earth as a universally accepted and enforceable moral code. It is an important historical event, that even this much has been accomplished. Otherwise, the individual human rights described are not remarkable at all. They are, in fact, similar to the laws and ideals of many modern states. Some of these existed in moral and legal codes thousands of years ago.

Another important fact is that the Universal Declaration of Human Rights is not a pronouncement of bona fide legal rights, but a declaration of wish-list rights for implementation at some fortuitous future time. Only a small percentage of UN member nations embrace and attempt to support all the human rights principles. This situation will undoubtedly change with time.

According to the Universal Declaration, it was set forth "as a common standard of achievement for all peoples and all nations." It was intended as a guide for "education to promote respect for these rights and freedoms and by progressive measures, national and international, to secure their universal and effective recognition and observance, both among the peoples of Member States themselves and among the peoples of territories under their jurisdiction." The Universal Declaration is not a legal document as it stands today, nor is it generally acceptable to both capitalists and socialists. The document is loaded with the terms *liberty, freedoms, equality,* and *rights,* as though these are widely understood and agreed upon. Human rights are watched over and advanced by the UN Commission on Human Rights, which was created for this purpose. At each major human rights conference, extensions and refinements are added to the Universal Declaration. The findings of moral ecology have not as yet found their way into the UN human-rights process. I shall give an example.

In the Universal Declaration Article 17 says, "The family is the natural and fundamental group unit of society and is entitled to protection by society and the state." The 1966 elaborations offer this addition: "Choice and decision with regard to the size of the family must irrevocably rest with the family itself and cannot be made by anyone else." Another twenty years has passed and this utterance is thoroughly out of alignment with the shocking speed of world population growth and the unpopular ecological fact that wanton breeding is becoming intolerable.

The language used in the declaration made sparing use of the word *property*, using it in but one of the thirty articles describing human rights. Conventional moral ideas, popular in 1948, were presented in the human rights articles. The importance of property, as defined in chapter 19, is nowhere recognized. We easily perceive the influence of Marxian socialism despite the elevation given to security, equality, justice, and freedom, which in the real world of communism and socialism are given a back seat. The rather legal style of the declaration lends it the appearance of political neutrality.

The purpose of this section is to define the term *human rights* and to illustrate a few of its uses. This has been done. An article-by-article critique of the contents of past versions of the declaration from the viewpoint of an ecology of morals would be time consuming and add little to our understanding of moral thought. What we learn readily from a reading of the declaration is that changes in human ecology over time requires us to alter our perceptions of many of the human rights as originally set forth.

Future revisions of the Universal Declaration of Human Rights will have to cope with hard new facts of human ecology. Serious attention needs to be drawn toward the responsibilities of nations and individuals to control population growth and the abuse of all natural resources, including our abuse of our own health and well-being, which can become an onerous burden on our fellow humans. In devising new rights laws, it is imperative that we balance what we want from society with what we can give to it.

We have now reviewed four species of rights: legal rights, which are prerogatives granted us by law; wish-list rights, which concern property and privileges we would like our government to protect, to limit and regulate, or to transfer to us at the expense of others; self-conferred rights, which might be simply described as acting on personal decisions or impulses; and human rights, which, until they become national or international law, are but noble, thought-provoking statements of the wish-list rights species.

Also, we have learned that the word *rights* is overused, abused, and has no definite meaning. It needs a qualifier. *Legal rights* has sufficient standing in law and public usage to be regarded as a useful term, but only when the two words are joined to distinguish this form of the term *rights* from all other usages.

What I have called *wish-list rights* is a term that refers to the future, whereas *legal rights* refers to laws created in the past that remain effective in the present. The declaration of a right tells us about a proposed law that some individual or group wants. All rights proposals are of the wish-list species. As a replacement for the term *wish-list rights*, use *proposed right(s)* or, perhaps, *fantasy-right(s)*.

THE RIGHTS OF SOCIETY VERSUS INDIVIDUAL RIGHTS

We have briefly surveyed the ambiguous realm of rights from the viewpoint of human ecology and law. My intention has been to show the implications of ecological moral theory for the analysis and criticism of rights phenomena. We shall now investigate one of the perennial dilemmas of political and moral philosophy: the so-called conflict between the rights of society and individual rights. I shall begin here with what I mean when I use the word *society*.

A society is a group of interdependent people living together in or under some kind of system or governing structure. Societies come in all sizes —tribes, communities, states, countries, and nations—with some being formed around a special, commonly held socioeconomic concern, such as food gathering, farming, fishing, and manufacturing, religious beliefs, and so on. When I use the word *society*, I am alluding to a relatively large, nonspecialized society or nation like the United States, other Western nations, or Japan, all of which possess a strong central government and numerous specialized, social groupings (societies) built on common needs and interests.

In the foregoing I have favored using the word *society* rather than its synonym *community*. This seems appropriate because the title of this section makes use of a popular phrase in political philosophy: the rights of society.

What exactly are the rights of society? A society, such as the United States, is composed of a body of lay citizens and a specialized organization responsible for operating the government according to constitutional law. The legal rights of all citizens, including members of the government, are determined by law. In theory, government represents society and undertakes the tremendous task of protecting the property of its citizens. This task defines the rights of society. Individual legal rights are conferred on all citizens alike. If citizens overstep the bounds of legal rights, they are in conflict with the rights of society.

A common idea in the nineteenth century was that society behaved like an organism. It was believed that society had a common will. Like the Hegelian state, society had a life and personality of its own. It could will, for instance, that government aim to protect the weak from the predations of the strong. The contention was that warfare went on within society between its rights and the rights of individuals. One problem was how far the rights of individuals should go in exploiting human and other resources. Society found in government its means of expression and of integrating its various parts. Also, it found in government a physician to diagnose and cure its ills. We can no longer benefit from the concept that society has a mind of its own that can speak for or make any other sense of itself.

Society, like individuals, has no natural rights. We must find within society itself and, more particularly, within its government the sources of its rights. In the proposal stage, rights can be initiated by lay citizens or by governmental administrative and legislative officers. The constitutions of modern states define the form, function, and boundaries of govermment's legal powers. The principal function of government should be, as we have observed a number of times, to protect the total property* of its citizens. The rights of individuals and groups in a society are all the forms of human behavior that their government is constitutionally empowered to permit. These are the legal rights existing in a society at any given time. It adds nothing to speak of them as the rights *of* society.

A nation-state is usually obligated by constitutional law to initiate and administer such general services to citizens as may be required for the protection of their primordial and material property. The more usual examples of such general services are lawmaking, law enforcement, and a system of justice; national defense; international relations; social welfare and education; public health; public safety and transportation; environmental protection; and a monetary system and the collecting of revenues to cover the costs of all the services and functions of government.

The services just described illustrate but do not cover all of the rapidly proliferating inventory of governmental efforts to guide and manage the affairs of our society. Also, we have here a partial inventory of what our society has come to expect from government; not merely the adequate protection of our property, but the fulfillment of an inexhaustible wishlist of socioeconomic innovations.

With the creation of each new right and entitlement, we increase the cost of government. Since World War II, the cost of government has outpaced its income. It is now clear that our federal government has oversold what it can accomplish. Among the results are a pestiferous annual deficit and a crippling federal debt that cannot be capped, much less reduced. Government remained within legal bounds, but failed to observe its ecological moral bounds.

Future taxpayers have been saddled with paying the principal and interest on this huge debt. This governmental encroachment on the property rights of present and future citizens is clearly immoral, as is the piling on of costs for new legislation that requires borrowing. No evidence exists that our federal lawmakers have plans for paying the national debt.

---

*The word *property* should be understood and used in the full sense of its definition in chapter 19.

Likewise, we see no earnest effort to reduce the annual deficit. It is difficult to refrain from concluding that the fiscal profligacy of government is streaked with fraud.

To further complicate the picture of big government, we have trained a large segment of our population to depend on government for the solution of all socioeconomic problems. This has engendered a kind of parent-child relationship between government and its beneficiaries. Either we become more dependent on government or more like its victims, depending upon the degree to which we feel we are either beneficiaries or plundered taxpayers.

Society looks to government in many ways. More demands for rights and entitlements are being made daily. A powerful group of congresspersons favors taxing the rich to help the poor. Congressional politicians vie with each other for identification with certain social programs, for constituency recognition, and for finding new sources of revenue. Adding to the demands on government are such unplanned events as economic recession, natural disasters, the AIDS epidemic, vast environmental problems and the unpredictable fact that, once people become addicted to social security rights and entitlements, it is difficult for government and politicians to wean them from dependency.

RIGHTS OF GOVERNMENT

A hard fact of the shifting American dream is that government reserves for itself certain constitutional rights: the right to tax individual income and business profits; the right to tax material property held by individuals and groups; the right to levy sales taxes, excise taxes, and import duties; the right to borrow money; the right, under prescribed circumstances, to confiscate material property, such as transportation rights of way; and the right to draft its citizens in service (primordial property) in time of war.

In the United States, most federal methods of raising revenue can be duplicated by every state, county, and town. To make tax burdens even more difficult to calculate, many hidden state and local taxes are included. For example, a state may be taxing insurance premiums, or requiring telephone companies to bill rate payers for special services designed to aid the deaf and blind. Cities may levy a bed tax, or a tax on certain kinds of businesses may show up on utility and cable TV bills.

Of course, the many taxes we rarely think of include: federal excise taxes, taxes on gasoline, alcoholic beverages, amusement, restaurant meals, and surtaxes. Then, still others are hard to connect to the cost of living, such as federal and state corporation taxes that are passed through to the consumer, and federal funding that is off budget.

Since the 1950s, all levels of government have been stepping up efforts to invent and exploit new forms of revenue to cover the costs of increasing expenses. Income taxes are only one facet of this broad tax picture. In 1988, the average middle-class couple spent up to one-half of their annual income on taxes of one kind or another. The largest share of their tax burden comes from federal, state, county, and city taxes. However, if we add the hidden taxes, we are surprised by their shear size, variety, and collective cost. How far can big government go without gradually destroying the freedoms, incentives, initiatives, productivity, and quality of life of the millions who carry the burden of the tax load?

GOVERNMENT CAN BE DANGEROUS

The predicament just described is a clear danger signal if seen from the vantage point of moral ecology. Whenever government becomes preoccupied with encroaching on, rather than protecting the property of its citizens, it has set itself on the immoral course of the redistribution of wealth and the establishment of socialism. We are now well on the way toward socialism. Among the proposals to catch more converts is that we already have social democracy and must now achieve economic democracy. Other signs of this trend are our frenzied drive for more and more rights, our government's wretchedly egregious search for more sources of revenue, and the pathological public reliance on government and its power, which itself is a creature of government.

Is government really exceeding the classical bounds of protecting the property of its citizens? Democratic government has traditionally been expected to respond to the voices of the people. Can democratic government ignore public demands for more rights and entitlements? Will the growth of new rights for large segments of society be granted at the expense of the individual rights of minorities? If the answers to these questions are in the affirmative, we can expect the disappearance of the problem of how to keep individuals from encroaching on the so-called rights of society. In its stead, we shall have a new moral and political dilemma:

how to keep government from encroaching on the private property of individuals.

We began by talking about the rights of society versus individual rights. But now we must contend with an entirely different concern: a quandary over the authority of government to control the property rights of its citizens. This subject is of tremendous importance to moral ecology. The only agency that is permitted by law to commit the immoral act of plunder is government. Any other agency involved in this act is regarded as immoral and criminal, but government can get away with it because government is absolutely essential to the security and stability of society. Further, our constitution places no limits on governmental taxation and borrowing.

RIGHTISM

Attention has been directed to the current proliferation of rights of all kinds, to the corresponding public hunger to cash in on rights benefits, to the law-making prerogative of government, and to the unlimited power of government to tax and borrow. These are the basic ingredients of *rightism*. Put another way, rightism is characterized by a body of citizens eager for benefits, a body of citizens earmarked to pay for the benefits, and a body of lawmakers who permit the transfer of property from the second to the first body of citizens. We shall move on to some observations of the moral status of rightism.

The nineteenth century closed with a struggle against profiteering monopolies headed by the ultrawealthy robber barons of American industry. This situation is the epitome of individual rights overrunning the rights of society. Congress came to the rescue in 1890 by passing the Sherman Antitrust Act, which was designed to encourage competition and stifle monopoly. The twentieth century is closing with a monopolistic government swamping the middle class in a sea of public debt and taxes. Are we in the process of learning that a democracy can endanger itself and society when its government races headlong into social programs that are beyond its means? Rightism may acquire the momentum to sweep government beyond the limits of its moral imperative, i.e., the protection of the lives and other property of its citizens.

Rightism is not waiting in the wings, ready to catch on. It is here, alive and flourishing. It enjoys considerable appeal. It presents a way to fulfill our hopes, desires, and aspirations without cultivating intellectual and moral discipline, without acquiring high-level skills and general education, without long-range planning and productive work, and without necessarily assuming social and economic responsibilities. Rightism does have a few drawbacks. It does take time, work, and money to get rights proposals converted into law. Proponents may spend hours in volunteer political activist work and, of course, they can vote.

A tendency of democratic government is to react affirmatively to public clamor for rights and welfare services. Voters do react favorably to legislation and initiatives that promise an economic reward of some kind, be it a tax saving, child day-care centers, car insurance premium reductions, or something vague like "equal opportunity." A proposed California initiative that failed to get on the 1990 ballot called for higher taxes on business property than on residential property. Businesses were to pay two percent more on assessed valuation of their property than were owners of residences. Money raised by the extra two percent was to be doled out to residential property owners and renters, and some used to create public housing. Authors of this initiative referred to their scheme as "fair share." This is a clear appeal to voters to grab someone else's money. Nothing is said about the impact of this initiative on consumers who indirectly pay the tax as businesses pass the cost on to their customers. If this is a harbinger of things to come, we can expect other legalized raids on property rights, and more off-budget funding of social programs.

In the United States it is practically impossible for the general public to keep abreast of rights and entitlement legislation, much less to learn about and keep track of the intricacies of administering the various programs. Details of the workings of these programs only come to our attention following a major scandal like the Housing and Urban Development fiasco of 1989. A half-century ago no one could have predicted the variety, extent, and complexity of rightism, nor could they have predicted the grip that all this has on our attention and thought or the tremendous cost. To make matters worse, we rarely learn what percentage of the costs of a program actually get to the intended beneficiaries.

Only government has the awesome power to confiscate the property of its citizens. This power is a continuous threat to the stability of society, including government itself. If operating ideally, according to moral ecology principles, government would confine its activities to its property-protection functions, and would pay for all costs of operations with money raised through unconcealed, direct taxes.

We seem to have lost our way. In the middle of the present century, our government began seriously to misinterpret its basic functions. It developed the grandiose self-image of a world leader, policeman, protector, and financier. At home it erected massive social programs. We were literally hypnotized by our inexhaustible power. Now we have played out the great morality game of power and politics, and all these wonders have been accomplished with the limitless power to tax and borrow, upon which the Constitution remains silent.

Rightism, as we have noted, is accompanied by increases in unwanted governmental authority to control our lives. It is unsettling to witness our nation, which began by wresting itself free of dictatorship, to now be on a course toward controlling its citizenry that is more stringent and detailed than those the colonies lived under in the time of King George. Further, despite rightism, the security of our lives and other property are no greater today than a hundred years ago. One outcome of the growth of rightism will be extended governmental control of and authority over our property rights, and hence, over our freedom. Still another example of rightism's danger to society is the fact that humans inherit the propensity for both social and individual behavior. It would harm society to stifle either of these biologically necessary human characteristics. The furtherance of rightism encourages the suppression of individualism. On this count alone we cannot afford rampant rightism and its attendant social conformity.

Many sources of help are available to those who wish to promote and serve rightism. Federal and state legislatures are well stocked with politicians eager to please constituencies by voting for wish-list rights programs. Rightism is a golden door of opportunity for law professionals who can draft and advocate rights-proposal legislation; the laws resulting from such legislation will provide lucrative work for our ever-burgeoning population of attorneys. Moreover, all prospective beneficiaries of rightism can be counted on to help, as well as all those who can gain indirectly, such as businesses, tax accountants, social workers, and political policy and advocacy groups.

During the course of history, it is quite likely that no government long existed that did not provide its citizens with at least a modicum of law and order. Additionally, at one time or another, all governments have spent the peoples' resources on wars and enterprises that benefited the ruling hierarchy more than the people at large. Such episodes can be traced from the days of kings and emperors to the days of dictatorships and our current socialist regimes.

Now, in the United States, rightism makes it possible to follow the same old pattern, by lending itself to exploitation by politicians seeking election, constituency loyalty, popularity, and influence. It also condones the attainment of economic benefits (equity) for one class of citizens at the expense of another. It is a new disguise for a form of socialism. Rightism slanted toward egalitarianism smacks of a throwback to primitivism: a naked power struggle for a "fair share" of the other guy's winnings or profits. Government, of course, could preside over the process, thereby assuring an equitable distribution of the spoils. From another angle, it can be seen that rightism encourages some of the least attractive attributes of human nature to come out of the closet.

Long before rightism has exhausted its potential for political mischief, environmental problems will occupy center stage for the human race. As the world population grows we will face horrifying competition for the necessities of existence. The dream of a society of equals will fade before our common perception of our danger. Frightening human ecology problems will arise, producing a survival crisis for all. The glamour of the petty rightism craze will go underground, and we shall be glad to forget it.

One thing of which we can be certain, the more governmental control of citizens' property grows, the more remote the attainment of freedom becomes. Freedom, a condition sought by everyone, is not at all well understood. The meaning and place of freedom in human ecology and morality is explored in the next chapter.

23

Freedom

Here is another word, like *rights*, that is hard but not impossible to pin down. We must face the task of understanding freedom if we hope to apply successfully the principles of moral ecology to conquering today's socioeconomic and political problems.

Freedom must be tremendously significant to us because Americans cherish the word and love to use it on patriotic occasions, especially at Fourth of July celebrations. We seldom attempt to fathom its depths. We speak of ourselves as the land of the free or as a free country; however, despite the fanfare, we show practically no understanding of what freedom means or is capable of meaning.

Are we ever free and independent from either our internal environment of self, our biological requisites and desires, our environment of others, or our commonly held and shared natural environment, the abuse of which can mean death to us all? If to be free and independent merely means to rid ourselves of something, to be shut of it, or separated or detached from it, then there are many entities and experiences from which we cannot be free or independent. Obviously, in this sense, we cannot be free and independent from the laws governing our organismic structure, the nature of our ecosystem, or our dependence on habitat.

In a historical sense, we use the words *free* and *independent* as synonyms. Thus, we can say, we fought a war to become independent of England so we could be free to rule ourselves, we fought so we could become an independent nation. We fought to become unrestrained, which is to be both free and independent.

It is difficult at this time in history to believe the magnitude of the colonists' suffering from the restraints placed on them by the English. The gratitude we still feel for freedom remains profound even though we are unquestionably far into the process of losing it. That we have so little awareness of how this is happening should be a cause of great curiosity, if not alarm.

Is freedom, then, just a matter of removing restraints, becoming unfettered from duty and obligation, having the appetite and means for worming our way through a mountain of consumer goods, or what we experience upon being released from jail? The experiences just cited have one thing in common; the removal of behavioral restraints. It is common to think of freedom as relative to restraint and various degrees of increasing or decreasing restraint.

According to this view, freedom is like a leash on a dog that can be shortened, lengthened, or entirely removed. A dog on a short leash has less freedom than a dog on a long leash, whereas, a dog with no leash is totally free. A dog without a leash, however, is subject to capture. If it is released, it is subject to the control of a new master. Suppose the dog is set loose in the wilds, would it not then be free? Hardly, it would face alone multiple needs for biological requisites. The dog itself might be claimed as a biological requisite by a predator. An animal will find its best chance of survival in the wild if it is part of an established ecological system of its species. This is certainly true of human beings. Ultimately, every living creature surrenders to death, a macabre freedom.

Perhaps we are born free. But free of what, to do what? We are born utterly helpless and totally dependent on the environment of others. However, we are born with powerful, physiological equipment designed for survival; to take nutrition, to fend off disease, and we quickly learn how to make our needs known. We may not have been born free, but we have certainly inherited a deep yearning, even lust for freedom.

THE HEART OF FREEDOM

An instinctual drive to be free is expressed by all animals and it seems to be integrated with all other survival mechanisms. No animal, humans included, tolerates for long any form of incarceration or restraint. Trapped animals will chew a paw off to escape a trap. Humans have been known to endure years of painstaking work to tunnel a way out of a prison.

What is this thing called freedom that we so passionately desire? It is not just freedom from constraint, but the gaining of control over our lives that we so strongly want.

What human beings want is control of their lives, their bodies, and their minds, and control of their belongings and other personal material property. Such antisocial behaviors as robbery, fraud, censorship, rape, hostage taking, slavery, terrorism, kidnaping, and murder are all common ways of losing control of our property. They not only constitute crime, but, more importantly, they are examples of the loss of control of property and hence freedom.

The definition of freedom that is most consistent with the moral ecology theory advanced here, is that freedom is a condition that exists for society when its members possess total control of their property and do not intrude on or exploit the property of others.* I do not know of any government that has granted its citizens the legal right to the full and complete control of their property. Such a right would, obviously, make it difficult for all government agencies to levy and collect any form of taxes. Also, quite obviously, we are not going to witness the sweeping changes in governmental theory and practice that would be necessary to bring about the right to the complete control of our property. However, I believe that this definition of freedom has important implications for renovating and advancing our concept of freedom, and that it will stimulate our thinking about morality in general.

FREEDOM AS AN ABSOLUTE

Freedom, as we have defined it, may be regarded as an absolute, which means that unless we have total control of our property we are not free. We have been used to thinking of freedom as relative to discrete circumstances, such as a series of rights to do this or that. If we think of freedom as an absolute, we have to think of ourselves as either free or not free. That makes it impossible to be a little bit free, any more than we can be a little bit infected with the virus that causes AIDS. We either have the disease or not: we either have freedom or not. Well, if we do not have complete control of our property, we are, according to our theory, not free in the full sense of the word. We do not know for certain that the human race has at any time enjoyed a state of freedom.

---

*See reference to Andrew J. Galambos, Acknowledgments, page 6.

During the first forty years of the history of the United States, its citizens came close to having total control of their personal property. Taxes were practically nil. The government remained true to its principal job, which was to protect its citizens' property. Gradually, Congress became involved in dozens of service and social operations, such as territorial expansion, transportation, westward migrations, world trade, the Louisiana Purchase, and the conquest and exploitation of Indian property. A concomitant of all this diverse governmental activity was that Congress discovered the political magic in the power to tax and spend. Our brief age of innocence came to an end, as did our pristine encounter with freedom.

While absolute freedom exists nowhere, it does exist as a moral principle of tremendous usefulness. A stubborn obstacle to the understanding of freedom, as well as other moral principles, has been our incomplete conceptualization of personal property. We must retrain ourselves to think of our bodies and minds as our personal property and to realize that everything we produce with our primordial resources, all our experience of living, skills, capacities, and talents are our personal property; and we must include all other material property we acquire morally. When we think of the diversity of our property, which is our wealth, we must remind ourselves that our ownership of this property is not guaranteed, nor, for that matter, is our freedom. If unchecked rightism will further erode our ability to control our property and, thus, our freedom.

DETERMINANTS OF FREEDOM

The major determinant of freedom can be found in Statement 1, where we are enjoined "to protect the biological requisites and all additional property of self and others without encroaching on the property of anyone." If we are not individually committed to protecting the property of others, how can we reasonably expect to secure our own property from the encroachment of others? Freedom has been slow to develop. It requires a high degree of discipline, for which we humans have shown but little aptitude. Freedom is not only an exciting concept, but a thing of beauty as well. It is not only an object of skepticism and fear, but of love and fear, making it subject to imbalance. Even when freedom for all is an avowed purpose of the state, as in the United States, there exists no dependable balance of the forces of freedom and anti-freedom. We cannot have freedom if we do not respect the property rights of others. This is a moral imperative. It applies to all of us. Exceptions would be inimical to the formation of a moral or sane society.

In Western nations, particularly in the United States, individual freedoms (rights) are a high priority, whereas this is not true of Third World nations, where coping with poverty, famine, and other socioeconomic problems leaves both citizens and governments little time or incentive to deal with individual freedoms. It has only been in the last two hundred years that humankind has shown conspicuous interest in freedom and individual rights, and in the codification of human rights. This movement has been paralleled by the rise in power of the modern democratic state, which is beginning to behave as though its citizens exist for the purpose of funding socioeconomic programs concocted by government, and, to balance matters, more and more citizens behave as though all their wants and desires can be gained through the multiplication of rights to entitlements conferred or mandated by government.

It is difficult to believe that congressional pressure for more social programs is motivated by other than political ends such as vote buying. Early rights legislation represented an expansion of freedom. Now the drive for rights is emphasizing the drive for economic benefits for both high- and low-income citizens. Attempts to "equalize" the standard of living is not in the interest of greater freedom or more operational democracy. It is hard to believe that congressional pressure for more social programs is motivated by other than political rewards, unless an ulterior motive is the destruction of what little we have left of a right to control our personal property. The forfeiture of freedom in an effort to achieve political and social objectives is a formula for the destruction of democracy.

We cannot be said to be free unless we are in possession of all our property. If we do not have possession of our bodies, we are slaves. If we do not have possession of our material property, we are impoverished and powerless. It is clear that we are not free unless our property is secure. We hate crime and injustice because they diminish our property, freedom, security, and peace of mind. Any encroachment on the property of another diminishes that person's freedom. We strengthen the condition of freedom in the world when we refrain from invading the property rights of others without first obtaining their consent. We cannot talk about morality and freedom without also talking about property. Morality and freedom come close to being synonymous terms. Without the concept of property there is no meaningful way to employ the terms *morality* and *freedom*.

When lawmakers at every level of democratic government approve a new fund-raising technology, recommend new and ingenious sources of revenue, or are increasing some old standby tax, they should suffer qualms about the injury they are inflicting on people. They should be thinking about the thousands of times during a year that old taxes are being raised or new ones initiated all over the country. Each one of these examples, large and small, represents a confiscation of someone's private property, and, collectively, a serious blow to our freedom of choice. And the legislative process of undermining our freedom never ceases. When did government switch from seriously defending our property to seriously plundering it?

An immoral exploitation of the environment is capable of bringing disaster to us all. Freedom in the use of common property—say, the sea or the atmosphere—is a misnomer. Freedom is a condition that exists when the citizens of a community have the right to the complete control of their property. Common property belongs to the group, not to individuals. Under these circumstances no one has the moral or legal right to control property, though all may use it. No one may abuse it as though it were theirs exclusively. As we have learned, the moral use of common property is a function of the state of the human ecosystem at the time we make use of the property. When it becomes necessary to limit our use of a form of common property, we can no longer avoid facing moral absolutism.

The frequently quoted communist doctrinal "From each according to his ability, to each according to his needs" is seriously flawed from the viewpoint of moral ecology. The first phrase violates the concept of freedom that each individual has the legal right to the complete control of his property. The second phrase insists on supplying biological requisites to all people regardless of their contribution to society or to the support of themselves. The literal applications of these directives to the whole of a society would guarantee its moral undoing.

The concept of freedom here advanced requires acceptance of complete responsibility for the self. Ownership of the self and derivative property is an active, not an inactive, occupation. We cannot expect anyone other than ourselves to accept responsibility for our property. The ownership of property requires us to respect and accept responsibility toward the property of others. This is what citizenship is all about.

Is freedom a moral imperative to a moral world? It seems to me that freedom is what morality is all about. We are talking here about the freedom to control our property. We realize that such freedom is not just around the corner. However, our vision of a more perfect freedom must begin with just that—a vision. We cannot assume that our nation is the final end product of evolution. A way can be found to establish a society that is completely free. The changes required in our system of government are not large and complicated. One necessary step is to bring law into harmony with the very simple principles of moral ecology.

If we wish to preserve our freedom, we must preserve our own safety net. To the extent that we relinquish our responsibility for caring for ourselves and our other property, we expose ourselves to the loss of freedom and independence. We are all vulnerable to loss and misfortune. Perhaps we cannot find a way to protect ourselves from some forms of bad luck. We must accept our vulnerability to danger and mishap as a natural part of life, since we cannot protect ourselves from everything that can happen.

When and if we ever win the right to be free, what we shall have won is the legal right to control all of our property. Winning this right would not give us the right to control anyone else's property, nor would it fasten on us any other category of responsibility. For example, being free would not give us the obligation or the ability to equalize human differences, or to rectify the other human vicissitudes of life. All misfortunes and other disadvantages attributable to chance should be ameliorated by privately owned insurance.

Insurance is one of the most helpful of all human inventions. It can be used by all people to protect their freedom by protecting themselves and all other personal property. In this way we can help protect society, our affiliates, associates, family, and friends. Government has proven unreliable in crafting and administering insurance programs. We should seek insurance from private, nonpolitically aligned underwriters when possible. Some of the losses due to bad luck must be—in fact, have to be—shouldered by the victims. In the event of natural disasters, it is logical for the federal government to render assistance to victims, as has been the custom for many years. Also, private losses due to crime should be indemnified by government as part of its responsibility to protect us from crime.

SOME THOUGHTS ON FREEDOM

In thinking about freedom, we must bear in mind that the word *freedom* does not have a broad, well-recognized set of definitions. Freedom is most often thought of as permission to move about, to come and go more or less as we wish, to make up our minds regarding personal decisions and, in general, to do just about anything we please so long as we inflict no harm on others or their property.

In the process of growing up, most of us noticed that we were gradually given more freedom to act on our own. This was usually accompanied by an increase in our responsibilities, which seemed proportional to the aptitude we demonstrated in learning and performing our responsibilities. The more important and welcome the freedoms were that we have so cheerfully looked forward to, the greater and more overwhelming were the conditions and responsibilities that came along with them. It turned out that freedom, like other highly prized goals, came with high price-tags.

We kept accumulating freedoms and responsibilities until it seemed that we had more of the latter than the former. More and more we thought about reversing the situation: unburdening ourselves of the exhausting work and discipline that inexorably goes with the heavy responsibilites of being a full-blown adult. As we grow still older, we are forced by one circumstance or another to reduce our responsibilities, and in this process we discover that we lose some of our former freedom and independence. Finally, when we have lost all capacity to assume responsibility for ourselves, we no longer have freedom—love and support, perhaps, but not freedom.

The newborn baby, likewise, has no freedom. It is completely at the mercy of its caretakers. It can make no demand for the complete control of its property. The safety of the baby as property is in the hands of its caretakers and the protective functions of the state. The appropriate education of the child is to teach it how to care for and protect itself. This is the chief goal of early education, and includes teaching the reciprocity of love and communication, the human relations facilitators.

Early in life we find that freedom is not always at hand. We also learn that our freedom depends on our respect for and care of the property of others. Certain of our behaviors seem absolutely necessary to our security and a sense of well-being. We learn from experience that it is necessary to avoid a whole family of behaviors called dishonesty: blaming others or making excuses for our harmful acts, bragging, exaggerating, lying and giving out other forms of misinformation. We remember the necessity of keeping promises, fulfilling agreements, and abiding by contracts. We learn over and over that part of the price of one freedom may include voluntarily giving up some of another freedom. Thus we see that sacrifice is sometimes necessary: necessity becomes the progenitor of freedom and morality.

Moral education should consist primarily in learning what is necessary for the optimal functioning of social life. I believe that we cannot know freedom until we first understand the nature of necessity. In chapter 6, I spoke of moral functions, such as people caring for each other, as derivatives of biological necessity. The preceding paragraph merely samples a tremendous body of human behaviors that are associated with more advanced stages of human ecosystem development.

To have a life at all, we must be able to identify the necessities of biological existence and master the art of their acquisition. This is the fundamental technology of life, and we are not free in any sense until this body of knowledge and skills has become functionally integrated with our awareness of self and our relationship to the complexities of our environment. The freedom to own, preserve, maintain, and add to our primordial or acquired property makes possible that integration of life and habitat we call the human ecosystem. We must understand the necessities imposed on us by our nature before we can fathom freedom (and morality).

We frequently are warned that when we express our freedom we must not do so by encroaching on the freedom of others. Such statements seem logical until we realize that we cannot encroach on others' freedom but only on their property. When we, even momentarily, disrupt others' control of their property, we are diminishing their freedom. What we must do in expressing our own freedom is to avoid encroaching on the property rights of others. This is simple to understand but not always easy to do. However, it is a basic principle of moral ecology.

When speaking about freedom we have to keep in mind that the concept of absolute freedom, a legal right granting to all citizens of a state the total control of their property, must be distinguished from the concept of relative freedom. Absolute freedom is not an actual legal right anywhere in the world. It has been introduced in this chapter to push back the narrow confines of our use of the word *freedom* and to enrich the possibility of new insights for moral and political thought.

We need to further clarify the distinctive uses of *freedom*. To say we have a right to speak as we wish is equivalent to saying we have freedom of speech. In everyday conversation, freedom is regarded as relative to a specific act in a specific situation, such as freedom of speech, of the press, and of religion, whereas, absolute freedom is a condition that could exist under ideal circumstances where all are guaranteed the full control of their property. In a state of absolute freedom there would be no further need for the concept of relative freedom. All individuals would be free to do anything except encroach on another's property and this would likely be viewed as the only immorality.

Freedom is about property. Therefore, it is natural to have some apprehension regarding the loss of property. It behooves us to be concerned about such a loss, or be prepared to accept the loss of our freedom.

We know that property is merely something that somebody owns. It is not the cause of evil. It is not intrinsically harmful. We can drop the disparagement of property and all past misconceptions of it. We can bid farewell to Marx's obsessive hatred and distrust of private property. (If not private property, shall we designate primordial property and its derivatives as public property?) Since we ourselves are property, hating property is not a particularly efficacious mental hygiene ploy. Our main reason for extolling freedom is that it provides the societal climate essential for the attainment, preservation, and use of property.

OBSTACLES TO FREEDOM

I have presented a number of vital subjects and problems and demonstrated how I would approach analyzing and interpreting them using moral ecology principles. My main goal throughout this book has been to explore today's moral frontier. I make no claim to any unusual knowledge of the socioeconomic and political subjects selected for moral analysis. The fields of inquiry open to such investigation are, of course, encyclopedic and beyond the scope of this book. However, we should find it possible to enter discussions of moral and ethical problems with considerable confidence.

We have briefly examined what it would be like to experience absolute freedom, something we can easily imagine, but not directly experience. We live with the freedom we have available, relative freedom, which is becoming more scarce rather than more abundant. Also, we cannot feel very hopeful of having absolute freedom very soon. Passing over these thoughts gives rise to questions as to what retarded the thriving of freedom as it was experienced in the earliest years of our country. No doubt an ingredient was the moral climate created by our daily violation of the freedom of Indians and slaves. Dozens of obstacles, impediments, and hindrances to freedom have already been revealed. I shall briefly review some of the more important examples that have previously been accounted for and a few examples of a tide of intellectual clutter that hinders the understanding and protection of freedom.

The following is a list of social and political ideas and practices that impede, hinder, and obstruct the realization of freedom in America. Most

Freedom 217

of the items listed have been with us a long time. We take their verity as a matter of course. The bland assumption that majority rule is a mainstay of democracy or that despite biological differences all individuals deserve equal economic rewards are examples in point. The following list is not complete, but rather a handful of instructive examples of obstacles that stand between us and freedom.

1. Spending beyond its means will eventually force government at all levels to confiscate more and more of our private property thus further downgrading freedom in many ways.

2. An example of deceit and failure of duty is the continuing violation by Congress of its own law, the Gramm-Rudman deficit-reduction law enacted in 1985.* Not once were the provisions of this law met between 1985 and 1989. As one result we continue to accumulate annual large deficits, adding to the loss of control over our economic destiny and hence our freedom.

3. Our government seems absolutely determined to invent new social programs using tricky, new out-of-budget funding techniques at the expense of the property and freedom of the middle class most particularly.

4. Criminal activity in governmental agencies and in private enterprise especially stresses middle- and low-income groups with higher taxes and inflation (examples: the Housing and Urban Development scandal, the savings and loan debacle, and overcharges by private defense contractors).

5. Neonatal medicine may be of great interest to medical scientists and will no doubt bring in its wake scientific findings and technical fallout of value to humanity. However, its tremendous costs are not yet known to us. A government mandate to care for viable prenatal infants twenty-five months or more of age until they are ready for a home outside a hospital may cost taxpayers as much

---

*The full title of this legislation is the Balanced Budget and Emergency Deficit Control Act of 1985. The intent of the act was ultimately to bring government expenditures in line with in-coming revenue. This was to be accomplished in gradual stages, while all means of economizing, improving management, eliminating duplicate functions of agencies, and increasing Congressional discipline were attempted. See U.S. Code, 1988 edition, U.S. Government Printing Office.

as 400 thousand dollars per infant. The greatest source of such infants will probably be natural abortions (miscarriages). Who will pay for this prodigality (see chapter 17)? Neonatal medicine exemplifies our passion to control nature and to satisfy our pretense to know God's will, not our passion for freedom.

6. It appears obvious to me that majority rule, which protects us from tyranny of a minority, can offer us no guarantee of the continuance of such democracy and freedom as we now have. A democracy committed to majority rule is capable of self-destruction. Our federal government is positioned in a precarious fiscal predicament where many of us are impatient to move ahead with social programs but find ourselves economically hampered in so doing. As a nation we are on dangerous ground. We have begun a covert practice of out-of-budget funding of social programs. If we can kid ourselves that we are not going any further into debt, we cannot be very serious about freedom. Should forthrightness and freedom ever be sacrificed to social programs?

7. In the business community there is a widespread belief that population growth is a necessary condition for economic development. This encourages population overgrowth, which is a threat to a stable economy and to freedom. Population growth already has passed its optimal level. From now on continuing population growth will gradually destroy both democracy and freedom.

8. The "equalization" of citizens' economic advantages: here is but one of many ways to do it. Government mandates private auto insurance companies to charge especially low premiums to poor car owners. The cost of the premium discounts to the poor would be spread over the rates charged to more affluent car owners. This welfare program would not directly cost the government anything. Morally, it would be tantamount to confiscating the property of one specific group of citizens and handing it to another as a gift. The benefactors, having little to say, lose control of their property and their freedom.

9. Are uncompensated property transfers ever judged as moral in the system of moral ecology? I think not. Once government condones various forms of plundering one class of citizens for the "benefit" of another, the process can grow without limit and

become an established norm with its own game plan and rules. All this state of affairs would require is strong support by a majority of citizens. Abiding by new rules of play for redistributing wealth will now be judged as "fair," while backsliding will be viewed as "unfair." Sweden has such a system of socialism based on a steeply inclined progressive income tax. If we in the United States wind up in a similar situation, we should realize now, well in advance, that we shall be creating a human ecosystem that will be inimical to freedom.

10. It is going to be extremely difficult to slow down, stop, and then reverse the ruination of our natural environment. This is a major moral imperative, and doing it will be a tremendous test of world governments and the international ability to cooperate. Stringent population reduction and control will be necessary. Freedom will not so much hang in the balance as it will increase in importance. As we learn what is necessary biologically and in terms of our human ecosystem, we will understand the natural practicality of moral ecology principles. We may then be willing to give up some control of our property. Freedom flourishes when we, in good conscience, commit property to such a beneficial cause as improving the state of the ecosystem.

11. In the case of primordial property, owner and property are one. All material property derived from our bodies and minds represents our biological need to bring useful parts of our environment under control. This is a fundamental process necessary for survival.

    What we create is an extension of ourselves into our biotic and abiotic environment. No logical cutoff point between the self and environment can be readily determined. The interplay of self, others, and our natural environment is the basic process of the human ecology system. The arbitrary schism between primordial property and all other kinds of property is unnatural and misleading, and has retarded the development of the life sciences, social sciences, and moral philosophy.

    It is human nature to seek at least minimal control of our supportive environment. Any natural, or man-made impediment to our desire and ability to control certain aspects of our environment is an obstacle to our hereditary passion for freedom. Our deep-seated passion for security is but a facet of our passion for freedom. We cultivate defensive behaviors in order to increase our freedom from danger.

Socioeconomic philosophers of the nineteenth century, including Marx, failed to perceive the continuum that exists between primordial property and its derivative material property. When we humans are extending our environmental reach, where do we draw the line and say this is where human biology or the human ecosystem ends? Is it out there as far as we can reach with a radio telescope or a linear accelerator? We do not know. If we separate primordial and its derivative material property into dichotomies, we should then have to describe a human organism that exists without an integrated ecological system, which is, obviously, not the case. This artificial schism between primordial and material property is the main causative factor in the failure of socialist economies and political systems. We cannot strengthen peoples' aspirations for peace and freedom by forcibly taking control of their property. Historical examples of this fact are abundant.

12. Crime is any encroachment on the property of others without their permission, and includes such acts as murder, rape, robbery, arson, and fraud. All crimes, without exception are acts against the property of others. Criminal activity infiltrates every branch of public and private life. Attempts by government and private agencies to control crime are one of our most costly public endeavors. Crime is sometimes big business operating quite openly, such as drug traffic (a business that is estimated to gross 150 billion dollars per year). Not only do American citizens spend billions on patronizing criminal businesses, but they spend billions fighting crime. All of this is a drag on society, drastically curtailing control of our property. On this basis alone we can rank crime among the greatest enemies of freedom.

13. War is an even greater enemy of freedom, today more than ever. Modern warfare is not only a struggle between highly organized mass-killing military machines of great and small nations. It also is part of the struggle that goes on everywhere between competitive and adversarial individuals and groups fighting to overthrow one another's power, to employ their own political power advantageously, or to defend a position of power. For example, we can

only understand terrorism as a genuine form of warfare and a bid for political advantage. Islamic jihad (holy war), the persecution of infidels, massacres, activist disruption of the property controls of the other side, are a few more examples of modern war. Consider the war between pro- and anti-abortion forces. This is no back fence squabble, but a cataclysmic war that will profoundly affect the freedom of one half of the human race.

The use of force and paramilitary action is said to be essential when persuasion and legal political resources have failed to make headway. The belief that a cause will be heard and influenced by jeopardizing or destroying the property of others is an illusion the human race seems incapable of abandoning. As long as we insist on the immoral control of the property of others through any means, whatsoever, we shall not know peace or freedom.

14. When the business community is mandated by government to carry out social programs like retirement plans, health insurance, pregnancy leaves, child day care centers, unemployment insurance and job training programs, we are simultaneously presented with a number of significant moral problems. Certainly such programs are not immoral if they are the product of voluntary employer-employee planning and funding, and if no party to the cooperative programs is forced or coerced to participate and contribute to the programs. When, however, government mandates that all business organizations administer such programs and pass the costs through to its customers, plenty of morality issues arise.

What we call free enterprise is transmogrified into a tax collection agency and redistribution system for wealth. So-called free enterprise becomes a social welfare agency. Those at the receiving end of entitlements become a new order of aristocrats. The owners of the means of production will receive, as they do now, a small percentage of profits, but they shall have lost a considerable amount of control over their property. Government will have considerable control of operations without ownership or risks of any kind. Owners and operators will have diminished freedom. The new aristocrats' interests will be represented by government. They may have no genuine freedom and may be taxed on their benefits. If such a system were applied rigorously and universally throughout our society, we could become a vegetative state without freedom for anyone. The great American consumer will be stuck with a tax of some kind no matter which way he or she turns. The government can take credit for the social welfare explosion without assuming any responsibility or tax costs. However, the plan may hurt the economy and leave businesses with no profits to tax.

This sampling of obstacles to freedom may be overly pessimistic. Even so, with the test of time, some items could turn out worse than depicted, while others exist as described. Some are illustrative fictions based on actual proposals. Taken altogether, they warn us of the twists and turns in the long road to freedom.

DEMOCRACY AND FREEDOM

For more than 2,000 years the word *democracy* has been associated with a form of government administered by elected representatives and responsive to the will of the people. It has also been associated with law, justice, and freedom. During the nineteenth and twentieth centuries, our democracy cultivated one of its most cherished benefits, a principle called equality before the law.

During the last half of the twentieth century, the political usage of the term *equality* has spread beyond its moorings in the law. Equality has come to mean identical sharing of practically everything. Egalitarians believe that people should be entitled to share in all the advantages offered by modern society regardless of their contributions to society. This new egalitarian doctrine is sometimes referred to as economic democracy. The label I gave it in the preceding chapter is rightism.

It is extremely unfortunate that the word *equality* was ever adopted by political philosophy and law. Equality cannot be a legitimate, scientifically defensible objective of any government. As long as the laws of chance exist as part of the natural world, we cannot expect people to be more than an approximation of each other. However, it should be an important component of a democratic government to treat all its citizens similarly, not just before the law but in regard to every conceivable opportunity for self development.

If we are egalitarian, we must perforce be prejudiced against even the most elementary facts of biological science: for example, individual differences. Taking such a position would seriously impair the theory of morality based on the findings of human ecology. We would then have little prospect of some day becoming a society, the governing institutions of which would be conducive to the emergence of absolute freedom.

Congress should provide more freedom. Political minorities should be free to go their way so long as they do not encroach on the property rights of others. We do this with respect to religious organizations and their beliefs. Why not also with such issues as abortion rights?

We tend to believe that our form of government is both forward looking and a model of freedom. We believe this despite the fact that it has crippled itself during the half-century following World War II. Paralyzed with debt and the illusion of supremacy, we stumble from one ill-conceived social program to another, funded with morally suspect and untried financing technologies. We continue on our way, careening toward a fate that shall be well marked by our progeny but perhaps forever unknown to us.

I have presented evidence in these pages that civilization is the organization of community life and of society to protect private and commonly held property. As this objective is established and pursued, all else follows: art, science, technology, education, religion, and government. With the exception of government, these are the monuments of culture, rather than its sources. When we perceive evidence of high culture, we can be certain that the protection of property led the parade to a civilized state. With the protection of property a living fact, the people are free, and with freedom comes morality and civilization.

The moral factors that tower over all others are love, freedom, responsibility, property, and profit (in the broadest sense of the term). For what other reasons would we regard life as worth living?

Index

Basic terms identified, 15-20

Competition and cooperation, 186-187
Conflict in human affairs, 184-186
Contracts, agreements, and promises, 182-184
Crime, removing profit from, 149-150

Ecological theory of morals, 77-78, 155
Environment: components of, 79-80; and the organism, 97-99; overuse, abuse of, 85-87
Equality, 18-19, 211, 213, 222
Ethics and morals compared, 16-17

"Fair" and "unfair" compared, 17-18
Fetal tissue research, 127-129
Freedom: toward a definition of, 19, 207-208; as an absolute, 209-210; and democracy, 222-223; determinants of, 210-213; heart of, 208-209; obstacles to, 216-222; related to the individual, 213-216; relative and absolute, 216

Gandhi's list of seven sins, 174-175
Government: dangerous aspects of, 202-203; its role in shaping morality, 33-34, 52-55

Hardin's Law, 158
Human nature: role of intellect and emotion in, 67-69; role of habit and belief in, 69-71

Immoral act defined, 157
Injury, hurt, or harm as immoral behavior, 19-20, 151

Killing and murder, moral ecology of, 131-134; euthanasia

226   Index

and, 136-137; legal problems of, 138; in revenge, 137; secondary victims of, 137-138; suicide and, 134-136

Law and morality, 33-34, 36
Laws of Hammurabi, 49-50
Life flow and life cycles: abortion, motives leading to, 114; abortion, pro-choice arguments on, 109-116; life, security of, 105; life, value of, 107-109; 117; moral implications of, 105-117; premature birth, 115-116; when life begins, 106, 108-109
Lifeboat Case, 96
Love: basic elements of, 164; romantic versus productive, 165-168; of self, 168-171

Majority rule, 177-178
Media headlines of our times, 32
Media word magic, 21-22
Moral behavior: degeneracy of, 158; love as, 164-168, 170-171
Moral behavioral factors: drugs, 59; genetics, 61-63; heredity, 64; hormonal imbalance, 63-64; nutrition, 58-59
Morality: basic understanding of, 154; biological necessity of, 41, 45, 57, 97; concept of identification in, 83-85; distinctly human, 99; as function of the ecosystem; 46-47, 156; key elements of, 159; and law 36; operational factors of, 42-43; origins of, 41; role of government in shaping, 33-34, 52-55; and sanity, 171; of science and technology, 99-103; science-based, 75-78; of sex drive, 120; understanding of, 154
Moral(s): act defined, 157; concepts ranked, 171-173; confusing ideas of, 80-81; crossroads in today's world, 27-29, 83; dangerous theories of, 175-178; development among primitives, 45-47; dilemmas of modern medicine and, 118-120; ecological theory of, 78, 155; ecology of killing and murder (*see* Killing and murder); education, 25-27, 35, 76-77, 125-127, 150, 214-215; elements as objective, 93, 181-182; and ethics compared, 16-17; expert, be your own, 163-164; linguistics, 77; by propaganda, 21-24; and psychology, 77; and sex, 16; and values confused, 171-175. *See also* Lifeboat case and Triage.
Morals, ethics, and related terms identified, 15-20

"New Age" concerns, 36-37
Nuclear threat, 93-94

Overpopulation: catastrophe of, 90-92; problem of human ecology, 89-93

Political terms misused, 178-179
Power struggles, controlling others, 94-95

Pregnancy, teenage, 124-127
Profit: from business transactions, 146-147; from criminal activity, 149, 151-152; expanded view, 146; from gains and losses, 148; immoral, 147; immoral though legal, 151; its place in human affairs, 141; motive as a moral element, 150; nature of, 141
Propaganda, effects on morality, 13, 21-24
Property: as biological linkage, 84-85; contiguity of, 152; as core factor in moral law, 84-85; damage from loss of, 151; government as protector of, 145, 149; immoral acquisition of, 155-156; importance in human ecology, 154; legal aspects of, 142-143; moral and immoral transfer of, 183-184; nature of, 141-142; our inner environment as, 143-144; people as property, 105, 143
Property, profit, and morals, 141-153
Prostitution, 123

Religion, origins of, 53-54
Right(s): basic nature of, 18, 189-190; of government, 201-202; human, 195-198; legal, 191-192; of society versus individual rights, 198-201; self-conferred, 194-195; wish-list, 192-194
Rightism, history and growth of, 203-206

Sanity and morality, 171
Self, proprietorship and management of, 168-171
Sex: and crime, 121-122; education for teenagers, 126-127; factors in childhood, 124
Sex drive, morality of, 120
Sexually transmitted diseases (STDs), 122-123
Supremacy of the state, statism, 180-181

Teaching morals, moral behavior, 25-27, 35, 76-77, 125-127, 150, 214-215
Ten Commandments, 51
Today's world at moral crossroads, 27-29, 83
Triage, 96

Understanding morality, 154

Value and values, 19
Values and morals confused, 171-173